FROM ZEROS TO
HEROES

FROM ZEROS TO
HEROES

THE STORY OF ENGLAND'S
2007 RUGBY WORLD CUP

GEORGE ROBINSON

ICON BOOKS

Published in the UK in 2007 by
Icon Books Ltd, The Old Dairy,
Brook Road, Thriplow,
Cambridge SG8 7RG
email: info@iconbooks.co.uk
www.iconbooks.co.uk

Sold in the UK, Europe, South Africa and Asia
by Faber & Faber Ltd, 3 Queen Square,
London WC1N 3AU or their agents

Distributed in the UK, Europe, South Africa and Asia
by TBS Ltd, TBS Distribution Centre, Colchester Road
Frating Green, Colchester CO7 7DW

This edition published in Australia in 2007
by Allen & Unwin Pty Ltd,
PO Box 8500, 83 Alexander Street,
Crows Nest, NSW 2065

Distributed in Canada by
Penguin Books Canada,
90 Eglinton Avenue East, Suite 700,
Toronto, Ontario M4P 2YE

ISBN: 978-1840469-39-4

Typesetting and design by Simmons Pugh Ltd

Printed and bound in the UK by Clays of Bungay

CONTENTS

INTRODUCTION

This book is a celebration of a great achievement, the English rugby team reaching the final of the Rugby World Cup for the third time in six tournaments. Mistakes have been made in the running of English rugby and the development of the national team since England's wonderful victory in Sydney in 2003, but this is not a book about those mistakes. This is a book which charts the team's progress, through the warm-up games, the difficult first two games of the tournament proper and then onwards and upwards to the final. I will leave it to others to criticise the supposedly mistaken leadership strategy of Brian Ashton and just say: how many other coaches would have given their eye-teeth to have been sitting in his place in the splendid Stade de France watching their team play in the World Cup final?

Of course, France is a lovely place and, with the odd exception, every game was played in glorious early autumn weather. The French organised the tournament superbly, and every town or city where games were played went out of their way to welcome the invading supporters. The French themselves have a sophisticated, mature attitude to sport. They try hard, can even be fanatical, admire skill and like to win. But if they lose, *C'est la vie.* It's only a game. Witness my two French friends after we beat France in Paris in the semi-final. Certainly one of them shed a quiet tear, but then it was off to the bars to drink champagne, first to commiserate over the French loss but then to celebrate the success of their English friends and wish them luck in the final.

I enjoyed reliving the great festival that it was through writing about it, and I hope you will enjoy reliving it all by reading about it and looking at the photographs.

Soon we will be preparing to go to New Zealand in 2011. No doubt the All Blacks will be favourites yet again – but, as always, the pressure on them to win, especially on their home turf, will be enormous. I worry a bit about whether New Zealand has the stadiums and hotel accommodation to cope. I am sure they will. There has not been a bad World Cup tournament yet. They just seem to get better and better.

This one was brilliant!

George Robinson
October 2007

CHAPTER ONE

Triumph in Sydney, 2003

In war: resolution. In defeat: defiance. In victory: magnanimity.

Winston Churchill

– 27 seconds to go –

It was 17-17 and there were 65 seconds to go. If, after all this, the scores remained level, there would be a five drop-goal attempts shoot-out. Perish the thought! Come on lads, one last drive. An England line-out and hooker Steve Thompson, whose throwing at times in the tournament had been frustratingly wayward, throws it unerringly to Lewis Moody at the back of the line. Moody back to scrum-half Matt Dawson, Dawson to fly-half Jonny Wilkinson, Wilkinson to centre Mike Catt, Catt's tackled by Australian Elton Flatley. Ball comes back to Dawson, still not near enough for a Jonny drop-goal, so Dawson breaks and makes 15 metres and is now close to the for-wards. Neil Back breaks and passes to big Martin Johnson. Down goes Johnson but the ball comes back to Dawson.

Are we close enough? Yes! Is the position right? Yes. Back to Wilkinson. There are only 27 seconds left. Boot swings, ball soars, everything goes into slow motion, everyone stops and watches, in the stands we all rise. The ball goes right through the middle of the posts. 'We've won! We've f—— won!'

Who shall I give the quote to? I think it has to be Clive (now Sir Clive) Woodward, who said:

'I feel ecstatic for every single person in a white shirt. It makes you feel proud to be English. We made many errors but we won. We won the cup, that's it. It was massive. I am absolutely speechless. It was just fantastic, unbelievable. The whole team was brilliant. It was an awesome night.'

It was an awesome night, and it would have been even more awesome – or perhaps the word would have been awful – if England had lost, because they were better than the Australians, and at one point they were leading 14–5 thanks to three penalty goals from Jonny Wilkinson and a lovely try from Jason Robinson, after some good work by Lawrence Dallaglio and Matt Dawson and a final pass from Wilkinson. Shortly afterwards, steaming towards the line, Ben Kay knocked on. It could have proved to be a vital mistake.

In the second half England let Australia back into the game. Elton Flatley, having missed two penalties in the first half, now kicked two and brought Australia within three points of England. Wilkinson then missed his third attempt at a drop-goal. Nevertheless, with seconds to go, England were still leading, though defending desperately. At this point, referee André Watson gave what proved to be a hugely contentious penalty against the England scrum. Flatley did not miss. The whistle blew. A game that England had seemingly got sewn up was going into extra time.

The England team, who by now must have been reeling psychologically, had to pull themselves together. They did, and within two minutes of the restart moved three points ahead again, thanks to another excellent kick from Wilkinson after an Australian infringement at the line-out. However, yet again England were penalised and yet again Flatley made them pay, 17–17.

Then those last 65 seconds. Strewth!

Steve Thompson, the England hooker, summed the game up rather well when he said later:

'I was sort of zombified, staring out of the team bus window, thinking, "this is going to be our day". Because we'd been together so long we knew what we were supposed to do. I know we conceded that early try but then we were just scoring points, making the score-board tick over, and in the scrum, even though André Watson kept pinging us, I thought we had the upper hand. We just felt more powerful. But the ref was penalising all of us: front row, back row, I think he would have tried to penalise Jonny for not scrummaging properly if he could have. It was ridiculous. When Flatley got that late penalty that was the only time, for a very short period, when we looked at each other and thought, "What have we done?" But then we got into a huddle and Jonno said, "You can think you've either just lost the World Cup or you can go and win it." When Jonny kicked that drop goal I had my back to the posts. But I could see him start to smile. And I knew. Because Jonny doesn't smile that often in a game.'

– 'I was worried about whether he'd live' –

Rugby at international level in 1987 was a totally different game from the one played just 20 years later in 2007. None of the teams, with the possible exception of the All Blacks, was professional. The daily allowance for the England team in 1987 was 35 Australian dollars (less than £20). In 2003, all the England team were professional, were paid more than £100,000 a year, and employed agents to look after book and newspaper deals for them. Alison Kervin quoted England prop-forward, Paul Rendall, in her excellent book, Thirty Bullies:

'We didn't take it seriously in 1987. I can remember thinking "as long as we have a good time, everything will be okay." Then we got to the World Cup and we couldn't believe it – the New Zealanders had been training. Bastards! Bloody cheats. They had matching training tops and proper coaches and everything. We'd never seen anything like it. It was as if they'd let us down – broken ranks.'

Mind you, Rendall was obviously not going to let international rugby interfere with his lifestyle. Jeff Probyn, who shared a room with him in 1987, said later:

'I was impressed with him, to be fair; this ability to drink all night long, sleep for an hour and then train for four hours in ninety degrees was quite something. The coaches were worried about how he'd play, I was worried about whether he'd live.'

Only 16 nations took part in the 1987 World Cup. They were divided into four pools of four nations and the top two in each moved into the quarter-finals. In the pool stage the winner got two points, a draw meant one point for each team, and a loser got zero.

England's first game was against Australia. They lost 19–6 and were very miffed that Australian wing David Campese was awarded a try after he had knocked on. In their second game, England beat Japan 60–7. Finally, England played the USA, whom they beat to qualify for the quarter finals. The other qualifiers were, predictably, New Zealand, Australia, France, Wales, Scotland and Ireland – and, not so predictably, Fiji.

England played Wales and lost 16–3, performing very poorly. I remember getting up early in England to watch it, and could not believe how inept they were and what an awful game it was. Wales went on to be annihilated by New Zealand 49–6 in the first semi-final. By contrast, the other semi-final is still considered to be one of the great World Cup games. This is how Alison Kervin described it:

The second semi-final was in great contrast to the first, in that it was a truly great game. Arguably, it was one of the greatest games of all times. Australia had Campese who scored his twenty-fifth try to become the highest try-scorer in international rugby, and France had Serge Blanco – a masterful, natural ball player who was quick-thinking and unpredictable but always brilliant. The two sides combined to produce a breathtaking finale … With two minutes to go, France scored one of the greatest tries of all time. They launched an attack inside the Australian half. Eleven players handled the ball before Serge Blanco, drifting up from full back, then belted for the line and scored in the corner. It ended 30–24 to France, and the disappointment was written all over the faces of the Australian players who had been so confident of reaching the final, they had already booked their flights to Auckland and hotel accommodation.

By contrast, and disappointingly, the final was relatively dull, with New Zealand grinding out a victory over the French. Nevertheless, the whole tournament was rated a success and everyone looked forward to the next one, which would be played in the British Isles and France. I remember organising myself to go to as many games as possible.

– 'Andrew's missed another penalty' –

England were a much better team by 1991 and prepared more seriously for the World Cup. They had just won the Grand Slam. However, their first game, at Twickenham against New Zealand, the world champions, ended in defeat 18–12. It was a poor game, littered with mistakes and no fewer than 27 penalties. Nevertheless, England made it to the quarter-final where they faced the difficult prospect of beating France on their home turf in Paris. England played very well and won 19–10. I remember walking out of the ground feeling very proud.

Next, England ground out a semi-final victory over Scotland at Murrayfield. For some bizarre reason, one of my close friends – and a very keen rugby supporter – had allowed his son's future in-laws to organise his marriage that day, and we had to endure the wedding service instead of watching the game. Nevertheless, we sat on the back row, listening to it on the radio. At one point, one of the bridesmaids fainted and I said: 'She's probably heard that Andrew's missed another penalty.'

In the end, the great – and usually utterly reliable – Gavin Hastings missed a penalty from in front of the posts in the final minutes and England squeezed home 9–6 to reach the final. Many people were critical of the way England had played on their way to the final, saying that their unimaginative, kick-kick-kick approach was a travesty of the game of rugby as it should be played.

The other semi-final, between Australia and favourites New Zealand in Dublin, produced a surprise, at least to most – victory for Australia. The great Zinzan Brooke was forthright about his country's approach: 'Let's be honest. We got our heads stuck up our arses. We picked the wrong players and they did the wrong things.'

With England in the final, everyone seemed to discover the World Cup. It was a big contrast from four years earlier. To an extent, England fell for the jibes that the Australians had been making before the game about not playing proper rugby and they abandoned the formula that had proved so successful in earlier games. The forwards dominated and the backs threw the ball around. However, they could not breach a sturdy Australian defence and, in the end, they lost a match that the forwards felt they could have won if they had stuck to the tactics they had used in earlier rounds. Jason Leonard did not pull any punches when he said:

'So why the f… didn't we stop passing it? Why oh why, oh why, didn't we think about what was going on, and change tactics? Marty Roebuck was dropping the ball when the kicks were aimed at him, but we stopped kicking it and started spinning it. We knew Campese's weakness was under a high ball, but instead of lobbing high balls at him, we took him on. Why would we ever do that?'

Paul Ackford, the England lock, would say later about the final:

'I think in hindsight we took the final lightly, not in terms of the way we played but the importance of the occasion.

'There has been a lot of debate about the tactics involved that day. My memory of it is that we went down to Australia in the summer with pretty much the same side that played in the final, certainly the same pack, and we got absolutely smashed up front. So we thought there was no sense in playing that way against a similar Australian outfit.

'That's the reason why we decided to move the ball more than we had done in the tournament. Our mistake was that we went pretty well up front in the first half and we should have realised that at half-time and reverted to type.'

The winger, Simon Halliday, added,

'I think I've got a more rounded view of it than some of the stuff of the forwards have. I've read some of the stuff that people like Brian Moore and Mike Teague and Jeff Probyn have said – "We got it all wrong on the day. We should have changed tactics." But we all agreed that the way to beat Australia would be to attack them slightly wider out, because we'd had success with it and we thought we had the better players. We actually did get through a number of times, but I think they had worked out what we were trying to do.

'I think a more valid criticism would be that we perhaps needed a mix of tactics on the day. If you see Australia flooding across the pitch, then you bring one or two moves back, for example. I think it wasn't so much that we made a blunder. We were right to do what we did. We did everything but score tries. I think it was just perhaps a mix of tactics on the day that we fell down on.'

Anyway, England lost a very close game 12–6. Australia were an excellent side who had lost only four of their previous 25 matches. The Rugby World Cup was the winner. The tournament was now firmly established in all our minds and became the focus for all of us. The Five Nations, destined to become the Six Nations, was all right but what truly mattered from now on was winning that World Cup.

– 'He just ran right over the top of me' –

The next tournament was in South Africa, a country that had gone through enormous changes with the release from prison of Nelson Mandela and the ending of apartheid. Yet again, the New Zealand All Blacks were the favourites, though many fancied the Springboks who would, of course, be on their home patch. As if their over-all strength was not enough, New Zealand brought a new potent weapon in the form of the giant, Jonah Lomu.

Scotland had to play New Zealand in the quarter-finals, and full-back Gavin Hastings remembers facing Jonah Lomu:

'When I lined him up, he just ran right over the top of me. Hell, I'd been around international rugby for nine years. I was 6ft 2 and 15 stone – not exactly small for a full-back – but it was such a totally different proposition to play against him rather than simply watching him on television. Until you actually faced him and witnessed first-hand that power and explosive-ness, that strength and size, you just had no idea what you were up against.'

England played Australia in the quarter-finals. There was plenty of needle left over from their 1991 clash in the final, and the game was extremely tight. Indeed, it went into injury time at 22–22 and, when England won a penalty just inside their own half, I remember one of the pundits saying immediately: 'Right, kick it into touch on their 22, win the line-out, back to Andrew and dropped goal. Thank you very much.'

And that is exactly what happened. England had beaten Australia. Revenge was sweet.

However, the next hurdle was a semi-final against the All Blacks including Jonah Lomu. England did not have to wait long in the match to find out what they were up against. After just three minutes, Lomu crashed through three attempted tackles to score his first try. He scored three more in a 45–29 drubbing of England. Rory Underwood maintains that England were wary of being mesmerised by Lomu.

'[We] didn't want to become embroiled in a discussion about him, because they had fourteen other good players on their team. We didn't want Lomu to affect how we played as a side. Our approach was to try and close him down as quickly as possible; half-stop him and then the next person could come in and help. For the first twenty minutes he got the ball in space and with time to run. He was like a howitzer and my brother Tony got swatted and dragged and scragged. But Mike Catt got trampled over too and, in fact, not a single player managed to tackle him. Gavin Hastings had got the treatment in the previous round.'

So, England were out and it was an all-southern hemisphere final between the Springboks and the All Blacks. I felt that South Africa were quite lucky to be there because France had missed a great opportunity to score a try under the posts in the final minutes of their semi-final clash.

Although the All Blacks, with the redoubtable Jonah Lomu in their midst, were favourites to beat the

Springboks in the final, the tide of history was flowing against them. This was the new South Africa led by the inestimable Nelson Mandela who was to me 'the Man of the Twentieth Century'. He had shown overt and constant support for his national team (and remember, South African rugby had been a bastion of the apartheid regimes) and was, of course, there at the final. New Zealand were not going to beat South Africa on this day – and they did not.

On to 1999, when the hosts were Wales. Matches were played all over the British Isles and in France, but the first game and the final were played at the Millennium Stadium in Cardiff. England duly got through the pool stage and played South Africa, the holders, in a quarter-final in Paris. I went to the game, and remember that I felt quietly confident. It was a close game but in the second half Jannie de Beer, who was playing only because of injury, kicked a succession of dropped goals one after the other, no fewer than five in the end. I had never seen anything quite like it. I remember thinking that it was not quite right and that that was not how rugby matches were supposed to be won and lost, an ironic thought in view of performances in the future by Jonny Wilkinson. Altogether, with penalties and conversions, de Beer amassed 34 points and South Africa ran out easy winners at 44–21.

– The All Blacks did not know what had hit them –

The 1999 World Cup will always be remembered for the astonishing semi-final between France and New Zealand.

France were given no chance. They had been playing terribly and had come bottom in the previous season's Five Nations tournament. To everyone's astonishment, France beat the All Blacks 43–31 in one of the great games of World Cup rugby. As everyone had predicted, the All Blacks were soon ahead and, early in the second half, led 24–10. Then in 13 glorious minutes France scored no fewer than 26 points. The All Blacks did not know what had hit them.

On to the final. The teams, France and Australia, were finely matched, and indeed the whole history of their contests was closely matched. Of the 28 matches between them, each had won 13 with two draws. In the event, the game was close until the last quarter when Australia ran away with it and won 35–12. France had failed to produce the flair of their semi-final performance against the All Blacks.

– 2003 – could any Englishman forget it? –

The 2003 World Cup appeared to be England's best chance yet of winning the Webb Ellis Trophy. Certainly the manager, Clive Woodward, was confident. After being asked why his team had blown five Grand Slam opportunities before achieving it in 2003, he said:

'Those defeats were important. We learned a lot from them. You can't win without defeats. Now, we're at the World Cup and we won't lose. We've done defeats, but we've also done winning, and we're very good at winning now.

'You could argue that the top four or five teams at the World Cup are roughly of the same technical ability, and have been coached as well as each other. What will determine the winner will be the team that can find little advantages in every area of play. It will be the team that has something that no other team has – the edge. We've spent seven years finding a way of doing all the small things better, all the things that will give us the mental edge. I have left no stone unturned, and neither have the players. No stone unturned. We've got advantages in every tiny little area of play and it adds up to quite a major advantage. That's why we will win the World Cup.'

The build-up was impressive. Of the 68 games played since Woodward had taken charge as England's first full-time coach, 49 had been won, 17 lost and two drawn. However, since the 1999 World Cup, of the 40 matches played, 35 had been won. Furthermore, England had not lost at Twickenham since 1999.

For once England were up there challenging the perennial favourites, the All Blacks, and they started their approach to the tournament well by beating New Zealand 31–28 at Twickenham in the autumn of 2002. They followed that up with a 32–31 win against the Wallabies. Next came the Springboks, and England walloped them 53–3. So the southern hemisphere teams could be beaten, though remember these games were at Twickenham. The World Cup would be in Australia. Continuing their build-up, England finally achieved the Grand Slam and followed it with a tour to the southern hemisphere in June 2003, where they beat both New Zealand and Australia again. Finally, they beat France 45–14 at Twickenham just before they flew off to Australia.

England won their pool matches easily enough, beating South Africa 25–6, Samoa 35–22 and Uruguay 111–13. England wanted to come top in their group. Otherwise, they would almost certainly have to play New Zealand in the quarter-finals. In the event, South Africa had to, and duly lost. There was much talk of the harsh training regime the Springboks had been put through.

England had a tough and close game against Wales. Just after half-time, Wales were leading 10–3 and England were saved only by the superb kicking of Jonny Wilkinson, who picked up 23 points in England's eventual 28–17 victory. Ominously, Wales had crossed the England line three times.

On to the semi-finals – England vs. France and Australia vs. New Zealand – which would mean there would be a team from each hemisphere in the final. Australia beat New Zealand 22–10. New Zealand were really beginning to look like chokers – favourites before every tournament but never winning after their triumph in the first, rather amateur, affair all those years ago in 1987.

Then England played France. The conditions were atrocious – strong winds and sheeting rain. Clearly, kicking was going to be critical, so it was Jonny Wilkinson versus Frédéric Michalak. Wilkinson scored all of England's 24 points with three dropped goals and five penalties. Michalak was not so effective, missing four of his five penalty kicks.

Right, we're in the final. Are we going to win? Woodward had no doubts. The rest of us were nervous. We should win, but would we? Australia were definitely not chokers. They knew how to win when it mattered. For Woodward, this was the culmination of all he had strived for. He had changed the whole approach of the hierarchy at England's headquarters. He had changed the mindset of the England players. On the captaincy front, he had initially chosen the tough and flamboyant Lawrence Dallaglio, but the flamboyance had won over the toughness and Dallaglio fell foul of a nasty little newspaper sting. He was succeeded by the equally tough and certainly less flamboyant Martin Johnson, who had captained the successful 1997 British Lions team. Johnson proved to be an inspirational captain, setting a great example by his masterly forward play.

However, as well as having the right captain, Woodward's master stroke was to insist on being supported by a management and back-up team. Every aspect of the game, on and off the field, seemed to have a coach or a manager. Woodward's approach was: this is now the professional era, so let's be professional about it. Finally, the players themselves, as well as being skilful, had to be fit. This was 2003, not 1987. He told them:

'I fully expect you to be in the best physical condition possible, ready to play your best rugby when you show up here. If you don't, you'll soon find yourself off the mailing list.'

They stayed on the mailing list, and, as we saw, brought the Webb Ellis Trophy home to England.

CHAPTER TWO

The Warm-up

Give us the tools and we will finish the job.

Winston Churchill

– A satisfying performance –

The first warm-up game, against Wales at Twickenham on 5 August, was a severe embarrassment to Wales and not very helpful to England. In a similar match before the 2003 World Cup, England had scored 40 points and the Welsh talked of not allowing anything like that to happen again.

In the event, England ran in try after try and the final scoreline was England 62, Wales 5. Wasps captain Lawrence Dallaglio said afterwards:

'This is the kind of England environment I recognise. If someone plays well, you go out and play better so he has to play better still when he next takes the field. It's how it works in successful sides. We haven't been successful for a while, but when I look around me, it strikes me that it's a long time since I've seen such talent in an England squad. With due respect to Wales, I'm sure we'll be tested in different areas in the forthcoming warm-up games against France. We have to be pleased with this effort, though. We exerted such control that Wales found it impossible to apply pressure of any description.'

The England coach, Brian Ashton, was less euphoric, saying:

'That was a satisfying performance. If someone had told me before the game that we'd win 62–5 and dominate as we did, I'd have been just a little sceptical. At the same time, I'm not thinking: 'Jesus, this is the team to win England the World Cup.' There were some breakdowns in communication out there that really annoyed me. We won't be able to mess up scoring opportunities against the French, because they won't allow us second chances.'

Match Details

Scores: 5–0 Easter try, 10–0 Easter try, 12–0 Wilkinson con, 17–0 Borthwick try, 19–0 Wilkinson con, 22–0 Wilkinson pen, 27–0 Easter try, 29–0 Wilkinson con, 34–0 Easter try, 36–0 Wilkinson con, 36–5 D. James try, 41–5 Dallaglio try, 43–5 Wilkinson con, 48–5 Perry try, 50–5 Wilkinson con, 55–5 Robinson try, 60–55 Tait try, 62–5 Wilkinson con.

England: M. Tait (Newcastle), D. Strettle (Harlequins), D. Hipkiss (Leicester), A. Farrell (Saracens), J. Wilkinson (Newcastle), S. Perry (Bristol), A. Sheridan (Sale), M. Regan (Bristol), P. Vickery (Wasps, capt), S. Shaw (Wasps), S. Borthwick (Bath, M. Corry (Leicester), J.

Worsley (Wasps), N. Easter (Harlequins).

Replacements: G. Chuter (Leicester) for Regan, 56; M. Stevens (Bath) for Vickery, 40, L. Moody (Leicester) for Corry, 71, L. Dallaglio (Wasps) for Easter, 58.

Wales: L. Byrne (Ospreys), A. Brew (Ospreys), T. Shanklin (Cardiff), G. Thomas (Cardiff, capt), D. James ((Llanelli), C. Sweeney (Dragons), G. Cooper (Gloucester), I. Thomas (Llanelli), H. Bennett (Ospreys), C. Horsman (Worcester), W. James (Gloucester), R. Sidoli (Cardiff), A. Wyn Jones (Ospreys), C. Charvis (Dragons), M. Owen (Dragons).

Replacements: G. Jenkins (Cardiff) for Thomas, 55; T. Rhys Thomas (Dragons) for Bennett, 52; R. Thomas (Dragons) for Horsman, 52; A. Popham (Llanelli) for Owen, 52; T. James (Cardiff) for Shanklin, 81.

– A golden chance spurned –

The second warm-up game against France, again at Twickenham, on Saturday 11 August, was more helpful.

The first half was close. France scored the only try when Pelous, equalling Phillippe Sella's 111 caps for his country, got past Josh Lewsey to score in the corner. This followed some good work by Aurélien Rougerie and a great pass by David Skrela to break through England's defence. In spite of this unconverted try and two French penalties, England led at half-time thanks to four penalties by Olly Barkley, three of them by no means easy. Mike Catt and Jamie Noon combined well in the centre.

The second half was close, with scrum-half Andy Gomarsall increasing England's lead after 15 minutes with a dropped goal. However, French replacement Jean-Baptiste Elissalde kept France within one point when he kicked a penalty from long range.

We were hugely disappointed when England failed to score near the end, after a great move following a break by Nick Abendanon made a try look certain. However, a desperate tackle by Szarzewski on Phil Vickery just short of the line saved the day. England would not win the World Cup if they spurned golden chances like that.

Worse was to follow when Sébastien Chabal used his considerable muscle to break through tackles by Abendanon and Lewsey to pass out wide and set up a try which was converted to the final score of 21–15.

As Brian Ashton said afterwards:

'Our execution let us down. You don't win big matches by blowing the three of four chances you create in the opposition 22, and it's not the way you win World Cups either. Am I convinced we have the players to address it? Yes I am, although I would add that some of those players were not necessarily on the field in this game. Finishing is one of the things we have to nail down before the tournament begins.'

Hmm. Where were Jeremy Guscott, Rory Underwood and Will Greenwood?

Match Details

England: Abendanon (Bath), Sackey (Wasps), Noon (Newcastle), Catt (London Irish, capt), Lewsey (Wasps), Barkley (Bath), Perry (Bristol), Sheridan (Sale), Regan (Bristol), Stevens (Bath), Shaw (Wasps), Kay (Leicester),

Haskell (Wasps), Worsley (Wasps), Dallaglio (Wasps).

Replacements: Mears (Bath), Vickery (Wasps), Corry (Leicester), Borthwick (Bath), Gomarsall (Harlequins), Wilkinson (Newcastle), Cipriani (Wasps).

France: Poitrenaud (Toulouse), Clerc (Toulouse), Marty (Perpignan), Traille (Biarritz), Rougerie (Clermont-Auvergne), Skrela (Stade Français), Mignoni (Clermont-Auvergne), Milloud (Bourgoin), Ibañez (Wasps, capt), Poux (Toulouse), Pelous (Toulouse), Thion (Biarritz), Betsen (Biarritz), Martin (Stade Français), Bonnaire (Bourgoin).

Replacements: Szarzewski (Stade Français), Mas (Perpignan), Chabal (Sale), Nyanga (Toulouse), Elissalde (Toulouse), Michalak (Toulouse), Heymans (Toulouse).

During the game, England had seemed to favour the mini-rucks, pick-up and drives rather than the driving maul for which they are famous. Whether this was to try to speed up delivery or to get away from the rather pre-dictable mauls I don't know, but it did not seem as effective a plan. In the event, the pack did not produce particularly quick ball and the English rarely troubled a strong French defence. Worryingly, England looked bereft of ideas of how to break that defence down. Jamie Noon looked good in defence but where was any flair in attack?

However, in spite of the possibly misplaced tactics, a number of English forwards enjoyed strong performances, especially Andrew Sheridan who gave Jean-Baptiste Poux a hard time. Matt Stevens did the same to Olivier Milloud, while Ben Kay and Simon Shaw both looked sound.

– 'We didn't do the basics well' –

The second game against France was played in the Stade Vélodrome in Marseille. Instead of their customary all white it was strange to see England come out in red. The New Zealanders have their haka to intimidate opponents before the kick-off. The French have one of the most stirring national anthems, the 'Marseillaise', and needless to say, nowhere is it sung with more passion and fervour than in the Stade Vélodrome in Marseille. Even for us English, it was very moving. We hoped it would improve the English performance as well as the French.

England went into the lead when Jonny Wilkinson kicked a penalty from 30 metres. He had already squandered a great opportunity to exert pressure by over-kicking a penalty so that he missed touch-down by the French try-line and the ball went dead instead.

This may have been a friendly (are games between England and France ever friendly?), but it didn't look like it on the field. Referee Alain Rolland twice brought together the captains, Phil Vickery and Raphael Ibañez, to lecture them. At half-time Dallaglio apparently voiced his frustration:

'It's a brutal game, but we were on the wrong end of a lot of the referee's decisions. I don't want to criticise Alain Rolland too much because he's going to ref us in the World Cup against Samoa, but the fact remains Simon Shaw got a card for a chest-high tackle, Phil Vickery got knocked out and stamped on all over and Mark Cueto was spear-tackled and we received nothing. There is no safety net now. We are into the real thing.'

In the second half, France moved comfortably ahead

before running out 22–9 winners. Ashton was moved to say:

'The biggest disappointment is that we didn't do the basics well. If you don't get the fundamentals right you've no chance of winning in France. We spent a lot of the game on the back foot. Last week the dressing room was angry because the players felt they should have won. Here, we didn't play well enough to win. I expected a lot more composure.'

Match Details

France: C. Poitrenaud, C. Heymans, D. Traille, Y. Jauzion, C. Dominici, F. Michalak, J.-B. Elissalde, O. Milloud, R. Ibañez (capt), J.-B. Poux, F. Pelous, J. Thion, Y. Nygana.

Replacements: L. Nallet for Pelous, 59; S. Bruno for Ibañez, 59; J. Bonnaire for Nygana, 61; N. Mas for Poux, 64; P. Mignoni for Elissalde, 67; D. Skrela for Traille, 72.

England: M. Cueto, J. Lewsey, D. Hipkiss, A. Farrell, J. Robinson, J. Wilkinson, S. Perry, P. Freshwater, M. Regan, P. Vickery (capt), S. Shaw, S. Borthwick, M. Corry, N. Easter, T. Rees.

Replacements: M. Stevens for Vickery, 40; L. Dallaglio for Easter, 52; P. Sackey for Lewsey, 62; J. Worsley for Rees, 64; O. Barkley for Corry, 73; A. Gomarsall for Perry, 79.

This is what some of the players said.

Simon Shaw: 'We're too one-dimensional and there's no interplay between the forwards and the backs. Either the forwards take it on or the backs take it on, there's no real mix.'

Dallaglio added: 'We didn't have a cutting edge, that's

pretty obvious. There's no second chance now, it's for real.'

And Josh Lewsey chipped in with: 'Playing like that isn't going to be good enough at this World Cup.'

Even Jason Robinson voiced his frustration:

'We have got to be realistic that we have to produce a big improvement in the way we have been playing, and that starts against the USA next Saturday in the first game.

'We are not going to take any team for granted. I'm sure some people think that the way we have been playing in the last three games, we will be an easy target.

'At times, there has been some frustration. As a winger, if you want to do what you do best, then you need the ball.

'I think there are a lot of good things to come out in the warm-up games we have had. But we certainly also need to improve some areas of our game and we need to get good balance. That has not happened over the course of the tournament.'

'The moment to book a last-minute holiday'

Brian Ashton recognised and openly acknowledged Robinson's frustration:

'Jason not getting the ball does concern me. I'd expect him to get more passes next time he runs out. When he's running free you've got to give him as much ball as possible. You don't need to create overlaps for him. One-on-one he'll make an opening and from 40 metres out he invariably gets over the try-line.'

Supporters were beginning to realise that the situation

was serious, almost a crisis. England had now lost 15 of their last 16 away games. They had just lost to France twice and failed to score a try in either game. They had also given away far too many penalties either through carelessness or lack of discipline.

England's ineptitude, and indeed ill-discipline, had been encapsulated by Mark Cueto when he almost gifted a try to France as he angrily fly-hacked his knock-on and the ball cannoned off Hipkiss. England conceded no fewer than 15 penalties and free-kicks, and were lucky that Jean-Baptiste Elissalde missed three penalties, Yannick Nyanga dropped the ball after crossing England's try-line, and Imanol Harinordoquy ignored Clément Poitrenaud when a pass would have resulted in a certain try. France's defence looked absolutely solid and England never looked like breaching it.

England's cause was not helped by the late withdrawal of George Chuter and the strong man Andrew Sheridan, who was ruled out because, of all things, an insect bite. Brian Ashton grunted something about 'the best laid plans of mice and men'.

And, on the pitch, there was further disruption to the England front row when Phil Vickery retired just before half-time following a bang to the head. In spite of these problems, we noted that, after scoring nine tries against an under-strength Wales, England failed to score one in either of these games against France.

Vickery's injury looked very worrying. However, he was diagnosed as having concussion, and said later:

'I'm fine, the head's clear and I'm feeling a lot better. Once I'd got some oxygen in the doc's room at the stadium I came round pretty quickly.

'It's not like the last time I got thumped in a club game against Bristol back in March. I did damage my inner ear that day and I still can't remember a thing about it. This was different. I can remember everything. It was so disappointing to come off because I was enjoying it.

'I know we didn't play well and I know the fans will be disappointed themselves. But, for me, there was a huge amount of guts and spirit on show. I know you need more than that, but if you haven't got that, then you're going nowhere. We can improve on that.'

Robert Kitson summed it all up in his match report for *The Guardian* by concluding:

If your enjoyment stems purely from English success, this is the moment to book a last-minute holiday in some far-flung location. Supporters of the red rose will soon appreciate how spoilt they were in 2003. Even Wilkinson is struggling to dig them out of the manure this time and the big win over Wales a fortnight ago looks more Pyrrhic by the day. No team has ever retained a Rugby World Cup. It is not going to happen in 2007 either.

As it happened, Jonny Wilkinson moved above the great Michael Lynagh on Test rugby's all-line points chart. He passed Lynagh's 911 as he kicked three penalties to put himself in third place behind Wales's Neil Jenkins and Italian Diego Dominguez. Of more significance was the injury to the England captain Phil Vickery. He was carried off just before half-time after a collision with Simon Shaw, who was himself sent to the sin-bin for a high tackle on the French centre, Damien Traille.

Unsurprisingly, the English team received a hostile reception in the rather forbidding Stade Vélodrome in Marseille from the 60,000 crowd. One benefit was the chance to acclimatise themselves to a ground where they would hope to play either Wales or Australia on 6 October.

– The squad –

Finally, Brian Ashton had to make his selection of the 30-man squad to represent England in the sixth Rugby World Cup.

Eight players from the original party of 38 were not selected (there had been an earlier cull from 47). To the surprise of some, Mike Tindall and Charlie Hodgson were two of the eight. The others were, among the backs, Nick Abendanon, and Toby Flood; and from the forwards, Kevin Yates, Danny Cipriani, Tom Palmer and James Maskell. In truth, Mike Tindall, having broken his leg in April, probably never stood a chance, and Hodgson had also suffered a serious knee injury the previous autumn.

Reliance on experience seemed to be a watchword for Ashton, which must have helped Lawrence Dallaglio and Mike Catt into the final squad. There were 12 players from the 2003 World Cup squad, as well as Simon Shaw who had flown out as a possible replacement but did not play.

It had been a tough call for Ashton, and he said:

'I have had to make some very difficult decisions in reducing the World Cup training squad to 30. I would like to thank all 47 members of the original squad who all put in a tremendous amount of effort into their work with us. Their attitude throughout has been first class. I spoke to each of the players who would not be involved in the final 30 yesterday, and they were all obviously very disappointed not to be included. But I stressed to each of them that they could be invited back if a member of the squad suffers an injury either before or during the World Cup.

'Mike Tindall has worked very hard to recover from his injury, and he was running last week. But it was agreed by the coaches that he and Charlie Hodgson, who is fit but like Mike has not played top level rugby for a number of months, could not use the final warm-up Test [against France the following Saturday] or the World Cup pool games as part of their rehab. Both of them have done everything that has been asked of them, and I wish them both well with their return to their clubs, and the other players who have not made the final 30.'

In many ways it was amazing that Lawrence Dallaglio was going. He had been a star of the 2003 campaign but, since then, had announced his retirement from international rugby, then changed his mind, endured a terrible ankle injury on a British Lions tour, struggled to hold his place at his club, and spent the whole of one Six Nations tournament on the bench and another not even being in the squad at all. However, his performances for Wasps in last season's Heineken Cup could not be ignored, so here he was, at 35, off on another World Cup campaign.

Chris Hewett, rugby correspondent of *The Independent*, picked six players, described three of them as the 'the old guard', and said England would be relying on them to do the business in France. They were:

Jonny Wilkinson
The face of the last World Cup, even if he was far from the key performer (that accolade went to Martin Johnson). Injury – or rather, an entire medical textbook of injuries – kept Wilkinson out of an England shirt for more than three years, but Twickenham hearts grew fonder in his absence.

Phil Vickery
His post-2003 career was seriously interrupted by injury, but he will travel to France next month as captain. In his prime, he was

just about the best tight-head prop in the world. Even now, at 31, he sets the tone with his fierce aggression in the darkest corners of the contest.

Jason Robinson

Mr William Whizz Esq scored England's only try in the 2003 final against the Wallabies, thereby capping a strong contribution that included a decisive break in the tight quarter-final with Wales. Like Lawrence Dallaglio, the Sale wing retired from international rugby and then had second thoughts.

And some of the new, in the defence of the World Cup ...

Shaun Perry

The Bristol scrum-half is no spring-chicken – he was 25 when England won the World Cup, a year older than Wilkinson – but until the West Countrymen moved for him two seasons ago, he spent his time playing semi-professional rugby. He made his Test debut against New Zealand last November.

Tom Rees

Still in his teens in 2003, the best open-side flanker produced by England since Neil Back emerged in the Midlands would have played in the last Under-21 World Championship but for injury. He made his first England start in the Six Nations match with France last March.

Mathew Tait

A 17-year-old wannabe when Wilkinson, alongside whom he would soon play in the Newcastle midfield, dropped the goal that ended resistance on that night in Sydney. An outstanding sevens player, he made his Premiership debut six months after the winning of the World Cup.

– Fear of the England scrum –

Meanwhile, coaches from South Africa – Jake White – and France – Bernard Laporte – voiced their concerns about the tactics of the England forwards. Laporte said: 'It would be nice if England scrummaged properly. It would be nice if Sheridan scrummaged properly. Then it would be a good contest.'

These complaints, aired openly at press conferences, came in spite of the directive from the International Rugby Board demanding that coaches refrain from voicing comments about technical issues in what might be seen as an attempt to influence referees.

The final squad for the 2007 Rugby World Cup was:

Backs: O. Barkley (Bath), M. Catt (London Irish), M. Cueto (Sale Sharks), A. Farrell (Saracens), A. Gomarsall (Harlequins), D. Hipkiss (Leicester), J. Lewsey (Wasps), J. Noon (Newcastle), S. Perry (Bristol), P. Richardson (London Irish), J. Robinson (Sale Sharks), P. Sackey (Wasps), M. Tait (Newcastle), J. Wilkinson (Newcastle).

Forwards: S. Borthwick (Bath), G. Chuter (Leicester), M. Corry (Leicester), L. Dallaglio (Wasps), N. Easter (Harlequins), P. Freshwater (Perpignan), B. Kay (Leicester), L. Mears (Bath), L. Moody (Leicester), M. Regan (Bristol), T. Rees (Wasps), S. Shaw (Wasps), A. Sheridan (Sale Sharks), M. Stevens (Bath), J. Worsley (Wasps), P. Vickery (Wasps).

Statistics on the squad:
Mike Catt, the London Irish centre, was, at 36 in

September 2007, the oldest member. The next two were Mark Regan and Lawrence Dallaglio, both 35. The youngest was Newcastle's Mathew Tait at 21.

No fewer than 14 of the 30-man squad were 30 or older.

There were 12 players who were in the original 2003 World Cup squad – Mike Catt, Martin Corry, Lawrence Dallaglio, Andy Gomarsall, Ben Kay, Josh Lewsey, Lewis Moody, Mark Regan, Jason Robinson, Phil Vickery, Jonny Wilkinson and Joe Worsley.

Dallaglio had the most caps – 79 – while Dan Hipkiss had just one.

Catt equalled Jason Leonard's record of being selected for four World Cup tournaments.

After a ten-day break, England assembled at Twickenham just before their departure for France. The bookmakers priced them at 36–1 against retaining their title. Not much money going on England then! Later, there would be many people, including me, regretting that they had not taken a punt at that price. After all, you wouldn't miss £100 but you'd certainly notice an incoming cheque of £3,600.

Donald Trelford, former editor of *The Observer*, wrote in the *Daily Telegraph*:

Odds of 36-1 against England retaining the World Cup are an insult, but some we can hardly complain about. The only consolation I can offer is that I got 40-1 on South Africa a year before they won the 1995 event.

Josh Lewsey, a veteran of the 2003 campaign, said:

'There's no one in the current squad who is not a realist. They know that things haven't been good enough. They know that our performance in Marseille was disappointing, a backward step … Nobody expects us to go really well, which makes it perfect for us to come up on the rails and surprise people. You won't find anyone in the camp who isn't in an upbeat mood.'

Brian Ashton felt the need to remind his team that they were the reigning world champions, saying:

'Pool D aside, the other seismic bout sees the testosterone-powered challenges of England and South Africa meet in Paris. The loser will face the Aussies, so expect the mother of all forward clashes. England are capable of winning this, particularly if Smit, the Springbok captain, has not got over his neck injury, but if both play to their full potential the Boks should shade it.'

Meantime, the 29 coaches of the national teams were all give due warning that the referees had been ordered to crack down firmly on dissent, foul play, crooked feeds and players using illegal padding. Paddy O'Brien, manager of the panel of international referees, said:

'We've made it clear that when a referee makes a decision, rightly or wrongly, the players have to respect it. We don't want to go the way one or two other sports have gone. A captain may only seek interpretation when the ball is out of play. We may not want our refs to be liked, but we do want them to be respected. I also have concerns about the number of coaches running to the media to make complaints. [Wait till you see what happens after the France/New Zealand game.]'

No sooner had Jonny Wilkinson arrived in France than he was struck down by a freak injury. If the spirits of England supporters were already a bit low, they sank even lower. Wilkinson had turned his ankle in a non-contact defence session on the Tuesday before the first pool match against the USA in Lens on Saturday 8 September. A scan revealed that his right ankle had suffered a lateral ligament strain. And it looked serious. Dr Simon Moyes at the Wellington Hospital in London said: 'If we are praying, I imagine he would be fit within three weeks, but it is more likely to be six weeks with an injury like that.'

Olly Barkley, the Bath fly-half, was brought in as a replacement for the game against the USA. Dick Best, former England coach, wrote in the *Daily Telegraph*:

The loss of Jonny Wilkinson for England's initial defence of the Webb Ellis Cup might not be such a catastrophe, without being disrespectful to the United States. We are all aware that the main event of these early exchanges will happen in six days' time in Paris against South Africa and his presence will be required for that game, though only if he is 100 per cent fit.

His replacement, Olly Barkley, 25, of Bath, who is not averse to a bit of publicity himself (off the field [this was a reference to a bit of trouble with the law at a recent wedding reception]), is a fine understudy and in many respects not too dissimilar in the way he plays the game.

In fact, Jonny and Olly are almost two peas out of the same pod. They both play further behind the advantage line than the connoisseurs would like, although Olly might attack the line more often.

– 'The pressure is on' –

And the pressures – in the mind, mostly – were building. England's captain in the successful 2003 World Cup, Martin Johnson, pointed some of them out. Talking about the expectations of the French people because France were playing at home, he said:

Interesting, isn't it? You know, I was happier being away from home in 2003 than I was at home in 1999. Everyone builds things, everyone wants you not just to win but to kick off with a bang. Everyone here is talking about the end of the tournament and what might be for France. All Argentina are talking about is a win on Friday night. By a point. The French team need to think like that. But they're not being allowed to. Lose to Argentina, and then they are into sudden death against Ireland. France might be able to handle the match. Can they handle the occasion?

It makes me laugh when people talk about New Zealand choking in World Cups or peaking between them. What are they supposed to do, lose games deliberately two years out? Mind you, the pressure is on. I was there on holiday in January. Every waking moment has been about this World Cup. There is no excuse for them not to be at their best. It will be won or lost in the head.

Former England forward Brian Moore gave his forecast in the *Daily Telegraph*. It was full of references to the Second World War – 'D-Day, beaches, landing of foreign troops, liberating the French, American landings on Omaha beach' – but also contained some interesting insights:

Only the beating of the All Blacks by the Aussies was a genuine surprise last time round; apart from that all the other results went to plan. No giant-killings, only a few nervous moments for the eventual champions against the Samoans and the Welsh.

Contrast the potential for upset provided by the draw and the form of the combatants in this, the sixth Rugby World Cup and you will see a competition that is truly difficult to call; and the better for it.

I defy anyone, other than the fervently nationalistic, to view their team's challenge without some real doubt. …

If there is any certainty it is that for the Rugby World Cup to be a substantial success, it needs the host nation, France, to progress far into the knock-out stages. The tricky opening game against Argentina is not the start 'Herr Flick', French coach Bernard Laporte, would have chosen. …

It's an interesting mix being champions, yet also underdogs. I think a lot of people have forgotten that we are defending the title. No one's ever managed to do that. So, what a massive opportunity for a team, that's been written off all over the world, to go out and do something like that.

There are quite a few players in the squad from 2003 and I'm sure it will have crossed their minds.

As they flew off to France, Phil Vickery, the skipper, tried to cheer everyone up:

'I don't want to be remembered as the captain who had to give the trophy back. I can guarantee I will give 110 per cent to keep hold of it.

'I am focused on playing for England and captaining my team. I will do that to the best of my ability.

'We must have no regrets. I hope no one in the squad looks back on the tournament with "if-onlys" or "could haves" because it is too late then.

'We must give everything we have got and hopefully we can spring a few surprises.

'The France game proved the level we are at is not good enough. But we are not far away. We will go to France and give a good account of ourselves.'

And Andy Robinson, former England coach, sacked the previous autumn after England had lost three out of four matches including a first home loss to Argentina, added his bit of encouragement:

I think England will certainly get to the semi-finals. If they do they certainly have the one-off players to get to the final.

I certainly think that New Zealand will be favourites and France look strong at the moment and you never write off Australia, but I've got a feeling for England.

So, England went into the sixth World Cup with this record in the tournament: They had played 28 matches, won 20 and lost eight. They lost to Wales 16–3 in an awful quarter-final in the first World Cup in New Zealand in 1987 and to France 19–9 in a third-place play-off in South Africa in 1995. They had lost to New Zealand three times – 45–29 in the 1995 semi-finals in South Africa when Lomu overwhelmed them with his powerful running, and in two pool games, 18–12 at Twickenham in 1991 and 30–16 in 1999.

Their points total was:

For: 957 (99 tries, 76 conversions, 98 penalty goals and 14 dropped goals).

Against: 458.

– At last, we're here! –

Finally, in early September we all move over to France, whether by car, aeroplane, train or bicycle. Some are destined for smart hotels and limousines, some are taking the opportunity to study France and the French in depth, others are going to come and go, either for a single game or for every one in which England are playing. That will be four for certain. We all hope it will be more.

The French themselves have a number of views of rugby. The elite intellectuals of Paris look down their noses at it, while others see the rugby players themselves as some sort of elite. Whatever, on Thursday 6 September there were firework displays in all the cities where matches were being played, and certainly there was a great deal of interest among the French population which presumably would grow if France did well and wane very rapidly if they did badly.

The previous Sunday no fewer than 9,000 people watched the Australian team practising in the Stade Yves-du-Manor in Montpellier, and 5,000 greeted the New Zealand team when it arrived in Marseille.

Zinédine Zidane, slightly bizarrely, following his moment of madness in the 2006 Football World Cup final, was still a national hero, and he rang the French coach Bernard Laporte, to wish the team good luck. Laporte said: 'He rang to tell me we are about to live a powerful but very difficult moment. The words went straight to the heart of our players.'

It's good to be here. France is a wonderful place and the French – most of the time – are a wonderful people.

CHAPTER THREE

First game – USA – Oh dear!

*Decided only to be undecided, resolved to be irresolute, adamant
for drift, solid for fluidity, all-powerful to be impotent.*

Winston Churchill

– 'Slow ball' –

At last, on Friday 7 September, the first match was played.
Traditionally the host nation takes part in the opening
game. Shock! France lost! They were beaten, and con-
vincingly too, by Argentina. Maybe this would be a World
Cup full of surprises.

Interestingly, especially in view of what happened later,
everyone said that France must win – and therefore probably come top of their group – because then they would
meet Scotland or Italy in the quarter-finals rather than
the dreaded New Zealand.

England's waiting finally came to an end in Lens, in
northern France, the next day. Lens is in the Pas-de-Calais
département and is a mining and industrial town with a
population of 37,000 people, largely working-class.

Immediately outside the town the views are somewhat spoiled by the many large slag heaps. It is in the 'black country' of France. The town suffered mightily during the First World War, being occupied by the Germans from 1914 to 1918 and losing half its population. The main reason for having a World Cup pool match in Lens was the famous stadium, Stade Bollaert, home to the equally famous Racing Club de Lens football team.

As we have seen, Ashton had already been forced to make one substitution – Olly Barkley for the injured Jonny Wilkinson. Otherwise, he had turned to the experienced old stagers. Lawrence Dallaglio, 35 years old, was selected rather than Nick Easter. It was only his second match for England in three years. Mike Catt, even older at 36, was picked at inside-centre to partner Jamie Noon. In the pack, the experienced Leicester lock, Ben Kay, was preferred to Steve Borthwick.

Joe Worsley was picked at blindside flanker in preference to Martin Corry, who was on the bench. Altogether, nine of the 15 players were over 30 years of age.

The fact that Olly Barkley was the only front-line kicker was a potential worry. Andy Farrell, on the bench, was the back-up kicker but it was noted that he had not done much kicking since he switched from Rugby League two years earlier!

Everyone was agreed. England would beat the USA but it was not a question of whether they would win but how. The forwards were bound to dominate, but how would England perform outside the scrum?

The answer, I'm afraid, was a very sub-standard performance. Furthermore, if ever there was a golden opportunity for England to pick up a bonus point for scoring four tries, this was it. They did not, even though they led 21–3 at half-time. England started uncertainly and, after 20 minutes, the score was still 3–3. And, in a way, England were lucky not to concede a try in a breakaway by the US team. They were saved only by a trip on Paul Emerick by Phil Vickery. The referee, Jonathan Kaplan, was unsighted and did not even award a penalty. As we shall see, a penalty and ten minutes in the sin bin for Vickery would have been preferable to what happened after the game.

In the 35th minute, with the Americans down to 14 men as Vahafolau Esikia was sitting in the sin bin, England finally managed to score a try. Josh Lewsey, playing his 50th international for England (he had led the teams out), made a break and passed to Mike Catt, who kicked for the unmarked Jason Robinson to catch and score. Just before half-time, Barkley scored and converted another try and England went in leading, rather luckily, by 21–3.

Eight minutes into the second half, wing-forward Tom Rees forced his way over for England's third try, which Barkley again converted. At this point we could have hoped for England to run riot and give themselves some much-needed confidence. It did not happen. Indeed, the only other score was a converted try by the Americans, eight minutes from the end. Dallaglio had been sent to the sin bin and while England were regrouping, USA replacement Matekitonga Moeakiola scored.

Press reaction in England was distinctly unfavourable. Former England forward Paul Ackford, in his Player Ratings in the *Sunday Telegraph*, awarded several England players only four marks out of ten. Of Mark Regan, he wrote:

4/10, less ebullient than usual and had trouble with his throwing-in on the odd occasion. Prompts questions over whether he should start against South Africa.

Phil Vickery (also 4/10) – Involved in the trip on Paul Emerick.

Unable to lead England from the mess they found themselves in. Needs to find something inspirational.

Ben Kay (4/10) – His hands let him down badly in general play and he did not have one of his best days. He's opened the door for Steve Borthwick to start against the Boks.

Lawrence Dallaglio (4/10) – An ineffective afternoon capped by his sin-binning. Massive indictment on England's perform-ance that he was forced to commit professional fouls.

The only player to whom he gave an 8/10 rating was Olly Barkley, praising him for his clean, precise breaks and even going so far as to say that he 'looks a more natural outside half than Jonny Wilkinson'.

He was also complimentary about Josh Lewsey – 'obvi-ously highly pumped and was England's catalyst for the first two tries' – and Tom Rees, who Ackford thought was the 'best England forward'.

Of the replacements, Ackford wrote: 'They all came on but no one made a difference. Andy Farrell made a good break in the final minutes but couldn't finish it off, and Mathew Tait flared very briefly. Much like England really.'

Some commentators were writing England off already, debating whether they would even qualify for the knock-out stages or saying that, if they did, then they would certainly be sent home by Australia in the quarter-final. No one gave them a prayer against South Africa.

Brian Moore was scathing, and wrote in the *Daily Telegraph*:

Of England's performance against the USA on Saturday, there is little to say that goes beyond inert. The maddening thing is that the basis of another poor performance remains the same – slow ball. Someone has to get the message through that the ball on the ground is not the stopping point. The opposition have to be hit back yards beyond, and laying the ball early and at arm's length is preferable to struggling for an extra yard. Until this is sorted it doesn't matter what combinations you pick, and where, because it will make no difference; not even a repeat performance from man-of-the-match Olly Barkley.

Former England captain Martin Johnson tried humour to soften the blow:

The United States are a powerful sporting nation, but not in rugby union. The sport there has a mostly amateur player base of 80,000 of which nearly 40 per cent is female. They've heard of the World Series alright, but not the World Cup, and if you asked most Americans what they thought of a maul, they'd say it was a great place to do their shopping on a Saturday afternoon.

– Vickery cited and out for two games –

This was all difficult to cope with for both the players and their supporters, and their mood was not lightened by the news that the result of the Americans citing Phil Vickery's trip of Paul Emerick was a two-match ban. This meant that Vickery would miss the vital games against South Africa and Samoa.

More bad news followed when Olly Barkley, perhaps the only person to play to his true form against the USA, strained a hip flexor in training.

In his team selection for the vital South Africa game, Ashton initially picked Vickery but, when he was banned, replaced him with Matt Stevens. Dallaglio was replaced by

Nick Easter and Martin Corry came in for Joe Worsley on the blindside flank. Mark Cueto's poor performance at full-back against the USA meant Ashton replaced him with Jason Robinson and picked Wasps' Paul Sackey on the left wing. Steven Borthwick made it on to the bench, as did Harlequins' scrum-half, Andy Gomarsall, replacing Peter Richards.

Ashton tried to be hopeful, albeit without much conviction. He told everyone that his new selections had been somewhat influenced by the poor performance against the USA, and added:

'When you see a performance like that you hope pretty fervently that you never see anything like it again. The back row was chosen particularly for this game. Obviously it could be dominated by the line-out so I thought it was important to have a big line-out presence. That's the reason for including Martin Corry. We did it against Wales and France and it was pretty successful.

'I'm hoping we scrummage well and that will give us the opportunity to do things from the base of the scrum which Nick Easter is particularly adept at. It gives him the opportunity to show what he can do with the ball in his hand.'

In the centre were Olly Barkley and Mathew Tait, forming a new partnership, and Wilkinson replaced Catt at fly-half.

– The criticism starts –

As if to emphasise what a number of people were thinking – and some were saying quite openly – about youth and speed instead of age and experience, Toby Flood, Jonny Wilkinson's partner at Newcastle, arrived as a replacement for Jamie Noon.

Will Carling, former England captain, admitted to being 'thoroughly frustrated' by England's performance against France in Marseille, but remained optimistic, saying:

The thing about England, and people might think I am absolutely nuts, is I still have a sort of optimism about what we could produce. The one thing we have found is that we suddenly have a pack of forwards who are physical again, competitive, combative. What we need is a little bit of pace and to find that link, especially between 10 and 12. The back three, Jason Robinson, Josh Lewsey and Mark Cueto, are class attackers. If we can just find that link again.

Carling managed to upset Lawrence Dallaglio and his supporters by saying that he felt he was a potentially divisive influence, and questioning the wisdom of his selection. When challenged on these remarks, Carling replied:

I think even his most ardent fans would have to say that he has been picked on reputation and hope rather than current form. My point was that he's a very strong character. He's a natural leader, so why not make him the leader instead of just having him in his squad.

I think he's the most experienced and dominant character in that group and you are not making him captain. That's the point that people seemed to have missed, including Lawrence. He's a natural leader. I am not sure why Brian has not given him an opportunity as captain. If Brian is picking an old squad for experience, then why not pick an old captain for this World Cup?

I am not sure that this was very helpful either. What would Phil Vickery and Martin Corry think of Dallaglio suddenly being made captain again?

Rob Andrew, former England fly-half and veteran of the 1987, 1991 and 1995 tournaments and now the Rugby Union's Elite Rugby Director, also put a brave face on England's prospects, saying:

'When we can get our biggest pack on the field, it's as big as any in the world and can be comfortable against any opposition. I'm very confident we'll give a good account of ourselves. The big games in World Cup tournaments are invariably one-score matches. And if you don't have your basics right for those sort of games, then you've got no chance. We've worked extremely hard to put the foundations back into the English game so that we can challenge anyone.

'I recognise that there are some issues with finishing and with creativity. That's something that has to be worked on. We need to score points in the tight games. The coaches simply had not had the time. The training camp was also a selection camp. The 47-man squad had to be whittled down to 30. That group has only been known for just over a week. Brian Ashton and his coaching team now have time prior to and within the World Cup to improve those other aspects. We're now ready to plan our way into the competition itself. Everyone is focused on the South Africa game. We know from our experiences in the summer what is required to face down South Africa.'

Brian Ashton gave the players a break – well-earned in the eyes of some, not so well-earned in recent weeks in the eyes of others – when they returned to England from Marseille. Questioned about the wisdom of it, he said:

'Yes, time is against us and we do need more time together on the field, but we also need a break. I felt on Saturday night that our energy levels dropped quite dramatically.

'We recognise that we didn't play well but there's been no flattening of morale. We're beyond that stage. The self-belief will only grow when we're together. I still think we can surprise people in this World Cup. It's not an impossible challenge at all. You just have to take each game on its merits.

'The lack of composure was disappointing. People didn't think clearly. And yes, the lack of creativity is also a concern. It's not as if we're just trying to play a damage-limitation game. We know we need to put other bits and pieces into our game if we're going to mount a defence of the World Cup.'

CHAPTER FOUR

Second game – South Africa – What a disgrace!

The Boneless Wonder. My parents
judged the spectacle would be too revolting.

Winston Churchill

– 'They can smash you with power' –

So, this was it. After all the talk and, by this time, a mountain of criticism, this would tell us the truth. Were England as bad as they seemed, or would they finally show that they could play in the way that they said they could?

Yet again, their preparations were adversely affected by injuries. A scan confirmed that Olly Barkley's hip flexor muscle strain was too bad to allow him to play, and he was replaced at outside-half by Andy Farrell, a position at which he was yet to play in rugby union.

Farrell made the best of it, saying:

'You tend to share the workload in that number 10/12 slot. That's the way Brian Ashton likes it. You have to take on a bit more responsibility at number 10 but it wouldn't matter to me what number I've got on my back.'

Ashton gave vent to his frustration about the injuries, saying:

'As usual with England injuries, there was no one near either of them. In situations like this, you wouldn't mind if there had been ten people kicking hell out of them.'

Mathew Tait had recovered from illness and was on the replacements' bench, as was scrum-half Peter Richards who would be employed, if necessary, as a utility back.

Nick Mallett in the *Daily Telegraph* tried to be hopeful, saying: 'Andrew Sheridan will need to have a massive game in the front row'; and 'Ben Kay will also have to perform a huge job in the organisation of the line-out.'

However, he feared the worst:

I also thought that England needed a big centre to hold up possession and not to initially pick one was a mistake – but injuries have brought in Andy Farrell and that may well work out in their favour. Yet with all their problems, I do not see how they will cope with South Africa's superior athleticism. As South Africa showed against Samoa, a team that England should not underrate, they can hit you with the pace of Bryan Habana – who is the sort of finisher that Jason Robinson was four or five years ago – or they can smash you with power.

Brian Moore, in his usual combative style, pulled no punches:

Playing Farrell at No. 10 seems to me to be a last desperate throw of the dice. Of all the positions on the field, the fly-half shapes the direction of the team. It is a hugely pressured position, full of technical nuances and angles; it is facile to compare it with the five-eighth position in rugby league, where Farrell has at least started games.

If you get it wrong the whole backline is neutered, in defence and attack. No doubt Farrell accepted the job with his customary courage, but this is no substitute for experience. The selection could be called bold, but is more like desperation.

The England back line that faces South Africa has changes in all three of its units; has had only a few training runs; and no game time. It is inconceivable that it will click from the first whistle and under pressure it is bound to be vulnerable, if for no other reason than unfamiliarity.

I cannot fathom the logic of moving Jason Robinson to full-back and dispensing with the services of Mark Cueto. To me, the most effective back three would be Josh Lewsey at the back with the Sale players on either wing. At full-back Robinson's evasiveness is lessened by the fact that he cannot disguise his runs as he can when he plays on the wing. Moreover, in any out-of-hand kicking duel, whether with Butch James or Percy Montgomery, he will come second.

Dick Best at least gave some constructive advice:

Kick, kick, kick. It might sound unbelievably boring, and it is, but it won us the World Cup four years ago. It was also Argentina's game plan against France last Friday and has been the basis of South Africa's for several years.

Mike Catt put a brave face on England's prospects, while admitting that they would have to make a big improvement over their performance against the USA. With regard to his partnership with Andy Farrell, after granting that they had had only one training run together, he said:

'I can only react positively. Whether it be playing with Faz at 12 or Wilko at 10 or Olly at 10, it's more or less the same job. I think Faz and myself are going to chop and change as long as we are clear what we are trying to do. We have just got to control the game with the help of scrum-half Shaun Perry. We are the main decision-makers and it is down to us to put ourselves in the right part of the pitch.

'We just need to tighten everything up. At the breakdown we need to be very secure. That is where America got us the last time. They just piled bodies in, whether legally or illegally it does not matter. They got away with it and we did not handle it well. We lost all shape. We can't afford to do that against South Africa. If we try to disrupt them in first phase, then that's the time to stop them, because once they get going they are difficult to stop.'

We could not believe the elementary mistakes

So there was all the advice and attempts to boost confidence. Would it work?

Unfortunately, and in spades, emphatically not! England suffered one of their worst defeats ever. As spectators we were stunned almost into silence. The Stade de France, built for the 1998 Football World Cup, is a fantastic spectacle at night and we had all assembled – it was a full house – with a great atmosphere. Everyone was on a high. Now, it took just seven minutes to go flat. Worse, there were even some jeers by the end. Some people even left before the end. It was symbolic of the whole game from England's point of view that, in their one attack that looked quite threatening, Jason Robinson was forced to pull up, in full flight, with a pulled hamstring. Jamie

Noon also suffered a knee ligament injury.

We could hardly believe the elementary mistakes the English made. The South Africans turned over ball no fewer than nine times, whereas England managed it just once. Shaun Perry, in the key position, was very poor but so were many others. For example, instead of the steady start so badly needed, England infringed at two of the first three line-outs and within five minutes conceded a try to South African flanker Juan Smith.

England came back but Mike Catt seemed completely at sea, missing a dropped goal attempt, kicking a ball into touch from outside his own 22 and then failing to find touch with a penalty. While all this was going on, François Steyn increased South Africa's lead with a penalty from 40 metres. That was 10–0 down after ten minutes.

There was a flash of inspiration from England on 20 minutes when they won a ball against the head, pushing the South African scrum firmly backwards. Unfortunately, instead of getting his line going, Perry kicked the ball into touch. South Africa themselves were by no means perfect and missed three dropped goal attempts. Nevertheless, by half-time South Africa had increased this lead to 20–0. They scored another try when they turned England over, the ball came loose, Farrell swiped a kick at the ball and missed, and Fourie du Preez snatched it up, made a lot of ground and passed to Pietersen for him to score.

Things did not improve for England in the second half. Percy Montgomery, South Africa's handsome full-back who wows the ladies, kicked three penalties and the du Preez/Pietersen partnership worked another try. Again, Farrell was involved as he and du Preez raced to pick up an erratic pass from Os du Randt. Farrell lost the race. It was the final humiliation. Furthermore, he had not covered himself in glory with his kicks at the restarts – and there were plenty of these – kicking long into the South

African 22 and consequently not applying any pressure.

And, of course, there was the loss of Jason Robinson with the hamstring injury. The way the 80,000 crowd stood and cheered him off suggested that most of them felt that this was the last game of a distinguished career. I noticed that the South African bench stood and applauded with the rest. (It was symbolic of the gentlemanly way the South African team behaved throughout the whole tournament. I'm afraid I could not say the same for some of the South African supporters.) He would certainly have wished for a better ending, and a better English display, if this was the case. However, watch this space!

Match details

England: J. Robinson (unattached), J. Lewsey (Wasps), J. Noon (Newcastle), A. Farrell (Saracens), P. Sackey (Wasps), M. Catt (London Irish), S. Perry (Bristol), A. Sheridan (Sale), M. Regan (Bristol), M. Stevens (Bath), S. Shaw (Wasps), B. Kay (Leicester), M. Corry (capt), T. Rees (Wasps), N. Easter (Harlequins).

Subs: A. Gomarsall (Harlequins) for Perry 40; L. Moody (Leicester) for Rees 53; G. Chuter (Leicester) for Regan 57; S. Borthwick (Bath) for Shaw 58; M. Tait (Newcastle) for Robinson 62; P. Freshwater (Perpignan) for Sheridan 79; P. Richards (London Irish) for Noon 79; S. Borthwick (Bath) for Shaw 55–60, 77–80.

South Africa: P. Montgomery; J.P. Pietersen, J. Fourie, F. Steyn, B. Habana, B. James, F. du Preez; O. du Randt, J. Smit (capt), B. Botha, B.J. Botha, V. Matfield, W. van Heerden, J. Smith, D. Rossouw.

Tries: Smith, Pietersen 2. Cons: Montgomery 3
Pens: Steyn, Montgomery 3
Subs: J. Muller for Botha 53; C.J. van der Linde for du Randt 61; R. Pienaar for du Preez 67; A. Pretorius for James 71; W. Olivier for Steyn 76; B. du Plessis for Smit 71; B. Skinstad for Smith 71.

Referee: J. Jutge (France)

Match Data

England		South Africa
0	Tries	3
0	Conversions	3
0	Penalty goals	5
0	Drop-goals	0
51	Tackles	97
7	Missed tackles	11
93	Carries	50
315	Metres	369
10	Defenders beaten	8
2	Clean breaks	6
14	Offload	6
33	Kicks from hand	44
16	Turnovers conceded	9
10	Penalties	8
0	Yellow cards	0
0	Red cards	0
8 from 9	Scrums	5 from 9
16 from 21	Line-outs	15 from 16
73 from 83	Rucks	41 from 41
61 per cent	Possession	39 per cent
62 per cent	Territory	38 per cent

What to do after that deflating experience? We went to our favourite bar after games in the Stade de France, the Frog and Princess just off St Germain-du-Pré; and, if I remember correctly, on to the Relais de Cambon behind the Ritz which stayed open until three o'clock in the morning. At that we'd had enough – of life in general.

– 'We cannot walk away' –

Brian Ashton tried to make the best of it. What else could he do? England were not out of the Cup yet, but the game against Samoa had now taken on immense significance. He said:

'I won't accept this was a worse performance than the one against the US last week. This was a much stronger side than the one we played last week.

'The whole context of the game was different. It was a more difficult challenge. If we had played against South Africa the way we did last week, they would have scored 80 points.

'We didn't play well in the first half but in the second half, we showed some resilience and some individuals stepped up to the mark.

'It's not been the easiest of weeks, that's for sure, but we have to get on with it. These things happen in professional sport and we may have lost another couple of players tonight. But we cannot walk away, we have still got to play Samoa next week.'

Martin Corry, standing in as captain for the suspended Phil Vickery, was his usual dignified and determined self, saying:

'The lads are shell-shocked but the most important thing is we now dust ourselves down. We will give ourselves 24 hours and then focus on Samoa. We gifted them pretty much 20 points which was very disappointing. After that we were playing catch-up against one of the best sides in the world. At least we showed some fighting spirit in the second half.

'Both sides realised they would have to work. But South Africa didn't work for every score. It was very frustrating. We are a side at the moment that is not playing to its potential.'

Paul Ackford was having none of it. He was apoplectic:

Very occasionally a game comes along which renders the normal emotional responses redundant. That match happened on Friday night at the Stade de France when England were poleaxed by South Africa. England were so inept, so woeful that the now customary reaction of anger or frustration following their dismal performances to date was inappropriate. This time the feelings went beyond rage to a dull ache of recognition that this World Cup has been calamitous for England's reputation around the world, that the players by and large are not of Test stature and that there have been serious shortcomings in the squad's selection and preparation.

And he obviously felt it was time to talk of all the problems in the English rugby set-up since the victory in 2003. It would seem to me that this was a little premature. Why not wait until England were definitely out of the 2007 World Cup and then try to analyse what went wrong? What had happened so far was two poor displays, the one ending in victory, the other in defeat. Two victories against Samoa and Tonga would see England qualify to play, most probably, Australia in the quarter-final. What England needed now was all the support they could get. Constructive criticism would be fine, even helpful, but harking back to 'no succession planning, an interminable conveyor belt of political squabbles and a sequence of coaches' was not going to further the cause of improving England's performance.

Furthermore, Ackford went on to take apart many of England's key players:

Why persist with Andy Farrell when at no time since he cheapened England's international jersey by having it handed to him on a plate has he looked even remotely like a Test midfield back? …

… Nick Easter, Shaun Perry and Jamie Noon are no more than average club players; Matt Stevens is too gentle a prop; Mark Regan's too engrossed in the mythology of the battle rather than the reality of it; and Paul Sackey and Tom Rees are young men with potential trying to finesse a game before they have mastered the fundamentals. Only Robinson, Andrew Sheridan, Martin Corry and Josh Lewsey have genuine international pedigrees and, Robinson apart, on Friday they were pretty much submerged by the ordinariness that accompanied them.

I am not sure how that was going to help. Perhaps it was an effort to shake those he was severely criticising out of what he perceived as their complacency.

– 'Northern hemisphere malaise' –

Nick Mallett in the *Sunday Telegraph* made a comment after the first two sets of matches in the four pools which seemed accurate at the time but would look premature a few weeks later:

The comparison between the southern and northern hemi-spheres has been harsher in this World Cup than any of the previous five. The southern hemisphere teams look young and vibrant, whereas the northern teams are old and stale. There seems to be northern hemisphere malaise.

Ackford was certainly scathing about virtually every England player except Jason Robinson, whom he described as 'heroic'. Most of the rest he lambasted:

Jamie Noon	– disappointing
Andy Farrell	– the experiment has not worked
Paul Sackey	– uninspiring
Mike Catt	– not a match-turner any more
Shaun Perry	– a shocker
Mark Regan	– doesn't deserve to retain his place
Matt Stevens	– not nasty enough
Nick Easter	– out of his depth

Gosh, the England/South Africa game was painful to watch. It took me back to the 1970s when Wales enjoyed their golden years. Going to Twickenham and having picnics in the car parks was fun but the games were depressing. Being in France is lovely, but this game was depressing beyond belief. How were England ever going to score if they could not get out of their own half? How were Catt and Farrell going to do anything if they never received quick ball? Only two other teams have failed to score a single point in a World Cup game – Namibia and Spain. No other reigning champion has ever failed to make the knock-out stage. There's always a first time, I'm afraid.

CHAPTER FIVE

Third game – Samoa – At least we're still in

Let us therefore brace ourselves to our duty ...

Winston Churchill

– Pick yourselves up –

The England team had to absorb a barrage of criticism from the press, their friends, certainly their detractors, and even from each other. Stories soon came out about full and frank discussions among the players and the coaches, with everyone getting any grouses or criticisms off their chests. The air was cleared, we hoped, and thoughts turned to a constructive way forward.

Ashton said:

'I take the ultimate responsibility but it's a collective thing as well. I've told them all that I have full confidence in them and will do so again prior to training. Our performances have dipped since those warm-up games against Wales and France.

Our performances have been nowhere near our potential. But I don't accept that we don't have the players. There's no question of players letting anyone down. They don't go out there to lose games or let people down. If we beat Samoa then we'll be back on track.'

Much was made, apparently, of the lack of England physicality at the breakdown. This had been noted in the USA game but the South Africans really exposed it.

Assistant coach John Wells said:

'I'm a big believer that if you don't win the collisions, it's hard work to win quick ball. We've got to start putting guys either through the half-holes or keep our leg-drive going a lot better than we have, to take a man full-on. The way the game is fought in these contact areas, you can't replicate it on the training pitch because the physicality is just too great. It's about winning the collisions and aggressive brutality at moving people off the ball.'

Ben Kay agreed with Wells, noticing how good the Springboks were in this area:

'It's got to be the clinical way they get a turnover, and this seems to be true for all the sides that are up there at the top of the rankings. This is where they set themselves apart. As soon as they seize on turnover ball, the New Zealanders do it very well as well, they will rip you apart. The key to these big games is not turning the ball over and that's where we made mistakes. It just proved the point that if you turn the ball over against such good sides, they'll hurt you.'

Samoa were next up and, under the circumstances, with morale somewhat shattered in the England camp, victory was by no means assured.

We all moved off to Nantes, which is located on the banks of the beautiful Loire river at the confluence of the Erdre and the Sèvre Nantaise. Fifty kilometres from the Atlantic Ocean, the climate here is very similar to the south-west of England. In 2003 the French newspaper, *L'Express*, voted Nantes the greenest city in France, while in both 2003 and 2004 it was voted 'best place to live' by the weekly *Le Point*. In August 2004, no less a journal than *Time* described Nantes as 'the most liveable city in all of Europe'.

Originally founded in 70 BC as a town by a Celtic tribe who called it Namnèt, it was conquered by Julius Caesar in 56 BC and named Portus Namnetus. It was then invaded by the Saxons around 285 AD, the Franks around 500, the Britons in the next two centuries, and the Normans in 843.

The city was deeply involved in the French Revolution, during which thousands of summary executions took place, mostly in the form of drownings in the Loire river. As calm returned, Nantes became an industrial city in the 19th century. Needless to say, it did not escape the traumas of the Second World War, when it was occupied by German forces. The murder of a German officer brought the retaliatory execution of 48 civilians. After being heavily bombed by the Royal Air Force in August 1943, Nantes was liberated from the Germans in 1944.

Over the years, both New Zealand and countries in Europe have been guilty of luring away the best Samoan players. For example, six of the Samoan team that played South Africa play their rugby in the English Premiership, and another two play in Scotland. Their coach, the former All Black flanker Michael Jones, highlighted some of the problems:

'We get our players from eight different systems so we've got a lot of work to do to bring them together.

'We don't try to turn them into a New Zealand rugby clone or an Australian or English rugby clone. We bring them back to the essence of who they are and that is based around pace, power and passion. We love to run with the ball. We love to bring our physicality onto the pitch. It's part of the warrior spirit. I can't bottle that up. I need to smooth over the rough edges but it would be remiss of me to train it out of them because that's the gift they've been given. We always talk about "playing to the gift".'

And if they were to 'play to the gift' on Saturday, England would have a game on their hands, because they were certainly not 'playing to the gift'.

Ashton recalled Joe Worsley instead of Tom Rees and urged him to concentrate on his big tackles, telling the press: 'Joe has shown he can make big, big tackles in big games, and if ever there was a game for him to step up in, this is it.'

– Jonny is back –

Both Jonny Wilkinson and Olly Barkley had recovered from injury, and both were picked to play against Samoa. Would Jonny be the man to turn England's fortunes around?

Ashton had no choice but to make some radical changes to the team that had lost so abjectly to South Africa. Jason Robinson was, of course, injured, as was Jamie Noon, who flew home. But fly-half Mike Catt, scrum-half Shaun Perry and flanker Tom Rees were not selected to sit on the bench. Lawrence Dallaglio was not recalled. Ashton stuck with Nick Easter alongside Martin Corry and Joe Worsley. In the pack, George Chuter was preferred to Mark Regan. Behind the scrum, the only person in the same place as in the starting line-up against South Africa was Paul Sackey. Josh Lewsey moved to full-back instead of Robinson and Mark Cueto came in to replace him on the wing.

Ashton, virtually forced into these moves, justified them as best he could, saying:

'Mark Cueto, I still think, has got a future as an international 15. He has not played a lot of rugby there. I sat down and talked with him, and he has not made the progress over games he's played quite as quickly as we would have hoped.

'Josh has been outstanding on this trip. His mindset has been excellent, and I don't have the slightest problem about him playing full-back.'

Certainly there were people calling for Ashton's head. Lawrence Donegan wrote in *The Guardian* two days *before* the vital Samoa game:

Even if England do make it through to the quarter-finals it is virtually inconceivable that any further progress will be made because the man expected to lead England to the promised land is the same man who has led England into this miserable cul-de-sac. As ludicrous as it seems now, Brian Ashton was heralded as a messiah when he took over from Andy Robinson at the tail end of last year. He promised a new era built on adventure, enterprise and candour. Instead he has delivered confusion, mistrust and dejection. Those who followed Ashton's chaotic spell in charge of the Irish national squad might have predicted as much, as might anyone who thought him more suited to the role of assistant than leader.

Donegan went on to suggest that because many of the journalists writing about rugby were former players, they didn't want to criticise someone they considered to be 'one of their own'. He also compared this with the continual laceration of England soccer manager Steve McLaren, suggesting that the rugby journalists' more gentle approach was possibly because rugby was more civilised. He concluded:

There comes a time when common decency steps over the line and becomes misplaced indulgence. English rugby has stepped over that line in the case of an incompetent coach. In short, it is time for the head of Brian Ashton, preferably decorated with a pair of donkey's ears.

– Two desperate teams –

England had met Samoa twice before in the World Cup. Both were bruising games which England eventually won, 44–22 in 1995 and 35–22 in 2003. They were actually behind in 2003 as late as the last 15 minutes before winning and, of course, going on to win the trophy. There were plenty of good players in the Samoan side. Mike Catt knew two of them well – Sailosi Tagicakibau and Seilala Mapusua – because they played with him at London Irish. He noted that both were 'fantastic runners and very strong players'. Far from their being handicapped by having many of the team playing in Europe, Catt thought they benefited from it.

Like England, Samoa had a lot to prove to themselves and their supporters. Their coach, Michael Jones, said: 'This will be a battle of two desperate teams. For us, there is no tomorrow. As for England, they will be jumping out of their skins.'

And it was going to be physical. Against Samoa it always was. We looked at Olly Barkley and Mathew Tait – well muscled and shapely – and then we thought of the Samoan centres and we were glad we would be in the stands, but feared for the safety of the England centres.

Of course, Olly Barkley knew one of their backs, Eliota Fuimaono-Sapolu, because he played alongside him at Bath. Barkley said, when asked about it:

'We know what to expect from Samoa but we don't really want to get into a big clash-bash battle with them. We don't want to give them the chance to put in their massive hits because that's what they like doing and that will only help them get their tails up. So we've got to move around. Their style of tackling is unique. They hit harder and higher than any team I've played against. You're aware in the Premiership that they might come in a bit late but it's something you learn to accept. If someone wants to take my head off, give us a penalty in front of the goal, then I'll take the three points every time.'

We all had our concerns about Mathew Tait and could remember how he had not looked ready for Test Match rugby when he played his first game against Wales. Since then he has been in and out of the team and, looking at his relatively slight figure, you could not help wondering how he would cope with the big men of the southern hemisphere. Tait himself said:

'It's a huge opportunity for me to put in the sort of perform-ance that says you can't drop me. It's been frustrating not to have had a regular role but it's up to me now to show what I can offer. From a physical point of view, I've matured. I handle myself better in that regard. I'm under no illusions as to how physical it's going to be. That's the nature of the beast. You've just got to relish it.'

Teams for Nantes

England: 15 J. Lewsey (Wasps), 14 P. Sackey (Wasps), 13 M. Tait (Newcastle), 12 O. Barkley (Bath), 11 M. Cueto (Sale), 10 J. Wilkinson (Newcastle), 9 A. Gomarsall (Harlequins), 1 A. Sheridan (Sale), 2 G. Chuter (Leicester), 3 M. Stevens (Bath), 4 S. Shaw (Wasps), 5 B. Kay (Leicester), 6 M. Corry (Leicester, capt), 7 J. Worsley (Wasps), 8 N. Easter (Harlequins).

Subs: M. Regan (Bristol), P. Freshwater (Perpignan), S. Borthwick (Bath), L. Moody (Leicester), P. Richards (London Irish), A. Farrell (Saracens), D. Hipkiss (Leicester).

Samoa: 15 L. Crichton (Worcester), 14 D. Lemi (Bristol), 13 S. Mapusua (London Irish), 12 B. Lima (Bristol), 11 A. Tuilagi (Leicester), 10 E. Fuimaono-Sapolu (Bath), 9 J. Polu (North Harbour), 1 K. Lealamanu'a (Dax), 2 M.S. Schwalger (Wellington), 3 C. Johnson (Saracens), 4 A. Tekori (Waitakere), 5 K. Thompson (Otago), 6 D. Leo (Wasps), 7 S. Sititi (Docomo Kansai, capt), 8 H. Tuilagi (Perpignan).

Subs: T. Fuga (Harlequins), F. Palaamo (Leeds), J. Purdie (Wellington), A. Vaeluaga (Bristol), S. So'oialo (Harlequins), J. Meafrou (Scopa), L. Lui (Moata'a).

Referee: A. Lewis (Ireland)

Former England centre Will Greenwood had some pretty harsh words to say by way of encouragement:

England's two performances [against the USA and South Africa] have lacked any authority, wit, flair, dynamism, nastiness or precision. Tactics have been poor, style non-existent. The tempo has been so staccato that it has stalled. Brains have not been engaged enough to implement a change of tack.

To get ourselves in shape for this important encounter we went for a day or two to Bordeaux which, of course, is in the centre of French rugby in south-west France. A number of World Cup games were played there, though not any in which England was involved. Bordeaux is a beautiful city and also, of course, a wine centre. Apparently, a significant number of Irish had moved there in the 19th century and became deeply involved in the wine trade. Certainly we found plenty of Irish bars. The burghers of Bordeaux had taken the World Cup seriously and had created a Rugby Village on the banks of the river. Even the art shops in the town had adopted a rugby theme. After a day or two enjoying Bordeaux it was off to Nantes.

Nantes is really a soccer town, but it had also taken the Rugby World Cup to its heart. There was a big screen in the Place de Bouffey and we enjoyed a few jars in the aptly named Webb Ellis and Co. bar. While we were watching the France vs. Ireland game on the screen the night before the England vs. Samoa game, some excited French supporters managed to shower me with wine.

On the day, we took a train out to the stadium and again there was a great atmosphere.

– An early try! –

After all the hectoring and advice, the team talks and team changes, Saturday 22 September finally arrived and England and Samoa faced each other on the rugby pitch in Nantes. First, England had to face down the Samoan haka which is probably more intimidating, or is intended to be, than New Zealand's own fairly fearsome battle song.

England knew they needed to start well and, to our great relief, they did, scoring through a try by Martin Corry after only 80 seconds. They were really gifted this try by Eliota Fuimaono-Sapolu's slow clearance kick which was charged down by Simon Shaw. Wilkinson converted and then dropped a goal to put England ten points in front.

There was not much in it for the next 20 minutes with both sides successfully converting two penalties, Wilkinson for England, Loki Crichton for Samoa. That was 16–6 as half-time approached. Then Wilkinson produced a bit of magic to set us all punching the air at last. He put Paul Sackey in for a try with a lovely little precision kick. His conversion put England 17 points ahead, though two more penalties meant the score at the break was 32–12.

So, could we now relax? Not a bit of it. Samoa came back hard in the second half. Another penalty was followed by a Samoan try when Mahouri Schwalger's grubber kick put scrum-half Junior Polu in for the try, bringing Samoa to within four points of England at 26–22. Furthermore, it was Samoa who were playing all the rugby now. We were back to biting our nails and fearing the worst again. Furthermore, the Samoans were being cheered by all the French in the crowd, who yelled *Allez les bleus.*

However, praise be for that miracle man, Wilkinson, who hit another dropped goal and a penalty (horror of horrors, during Samoa's supremacy period he missed with a relatively easy penalty kick). And then in the last ten minutes Corry went over for his second try and Sackey made a superb outside break for his second try. The final score line of 44–22 was good to look at, but we had to admit it rather flattered England. The win had certainly not been that comfortable.

After the game, the Samoans – after their usual prayer session – did a lap of honour, and it was noticeable that most of the English supporters stayed and applauded. Then we repaired to our Irish bar and had to suffer the ubiquitous English Premier League soccer on the big screen.

Nevertheless, we had won and everyone calmed down a bit from the hysteria of a week earlier. Paul Ackford was prepared to give sixes and sevens out of ten to most of the players, compared with twos and threes after the South African game. Poor Mathew Tait received only a five and this comment:

Didn't shrink from the physical stuff but struggled a couple of times in the tackle. Did not bring the creativity England sought.

Only one player received eight out of ten and that was Josh Lewsey, with a succinct 'Solid at the back'.

Of course, the headlines everywhere were praising Wilkinson and saying how his return had rescued England from impending disaster. Ackford was more critical: 'Missed Alesana Tuilai early on but was a steadying influence even if his kicking was miles too long. Kept the scoreboard moving.'

In retrospect, one of the most encouraging performances was that of Andy Gomarsall. Not as physically robust
as Shaun Perry, Gomarsall improved England's speed of
delivery of the ball by a country mile compared with the
South African game. Sackey scoring two tries was also significant. Apparently in the critical analysis the previous
week, England decided to try to play with more width,
and certainly Cueto and Sackey received more ball than
the wings had in the opening two games.

However, big games are almost invariably won or lost
up front or, to put it another way, you have to work mira-
cles outside if your forwards are not on top. In this game
they were, with the flankers trying to find space rather
than just running into their opposite number. Nick Easter
enjoyed a particularly strong game in this regard and, of
course, Martin Corry scored not one, but two tries.

– 'Join-the-dots rugby' –

However, there was still plenty to worry about. Apparently,
in the heart-to-heart (or was it confrontation?) after the
Springbok defeat, a number of players said they were
uncomfortable thinking for themselves. A player who did
not want to be named said:

'For the past few weeks we played with a style that was based
around looking up and seeing where the spaces were. It's very
difficult to get your running lines sorted when you don't know
where or to whom the ball is going. In training before the
Samoa game we simplified our structure. The emphasis was on
communicating which channels we were hitting, who was hitting them, which guys were going into the breakdown and

which guys were hanging back for the next phase. We've tightened up what we were doing. It's a bit more regimented.'

Paul Ackford was scathing about this approach. In the *Sunday Telegraph* he described it as 'Join-the-dots rugby' and said it was no wonder that Ashton had been a bit tetchy of late, as his philosophy of how rugby should be played – and which he had been trying to get the England team to adopt – had been 'thrown back in his face'.

It was reported later that England fly-half Olly Barkley had said to Brian Ashton: 'Look Brian, nobody's got a f— clue how we are supposed to be playing here. If you asked the 15 players who played against South Africa to write down the game plan, you'd get 15 different messages.'

Not that Ackford was letting Ashton off the hook. He went on to criticise him severely, saying:

Last week saw the 100th change to an England side in the 13 matches since he's been in charge ... that's an awful lot of indecision. Ashton's handling of Mark Cueto, first a full-back, now a wing, and Tom Rees initially portrayed as England's openside apostle then abruptly excommunicated, has been execrable ... There is no doubt he [Ashton] has been flaky under fire.

Martin Johnson, in assessing the games in the Sunday Telegraph, injected some good humorous comments:

Ever since the 2003 World Cup, there has been a widespread belief in England that the actor who played the bloke in the Milk Tray advert, who abseiled from cliff tops, swam several oceans, and finally flew in through a bedroom window merely to slip a box of chocolates under a lady's pillow, was none other than our Jonny.

So, as Samoa laid siege to the England try-line only four points behind with 12 minutes to go, we were thinking: 'It's not looking good, but our hero will arrive any minute to make everything better.'

And indeed Jonny was there – with his dropped goal and long-range penalty – although he had suffered a dangerously high tackle from Samoan centre Brian Lima.

Match Data

England	44–22	Samoa
4	Tries	1
3	Conversions	1
4	Penalty goals	5
2	Drop-goals	0
59%	Possession	41%
57%	Territory	43%
61	Tackles	75
7	Missed tackles	17
78	Carries	66
12	Turnovers conceded	12
10	Penalties conceded	10
6/6	Scrums won	9/9
7/9	Line-outs won	12/14
74/79	Rucks/mauls won	62/63
0	Yellow cards	0
0	Red cards	0

Scores:
First half: 5–0 Corry try, 7–0 Wilkinson con, 10–0 Wilkinson dg, 10–3 Crichton pen, 10–6 Crichton pen, 13–6 Wilkinson pen, 21–6 Sackey try, 23–6 Wilkinson con,

23–9 Crichton pen, 23–12 Crichton pen.

Second half: 23–15 Crichton pen, 26–15 Wilkinson pen, 26–20 Polu try, 26–22 Crichton con, 29–22 Wilkinson dg, 32–22 Wilkinson pen, 37–22 Corry try, 39–22 Wilkinson con, 44–22 Sackey try.

CHAPTER SIX

Fourth game –
Tonga – Improving

This is not the end. It is not even the beginning of the end.
But it is, perhaps, the end of the beginning.

Winston Churchill

– Tonga – not like 1999 –

England had been concerned about playing Samoa and, as we all saw, with plenty of justification. With the score at 26–22 and Samoa attacking with 12 minutes to go, many of us were convinced that England were going to lose. Now, they needed to be just as concerned about playing Tonga. Tonga had beaten Samoa and the USA and had earned a bonus point playing South Africa. A draw, therefore, would make Tonga runners-up in their pool and the England squad would be on their way home. England had to win to go through to the quarter-finals.

England will have noted how Tonga gave South Africa a big fright when they only just lost 30–25. Springboks coach Jake White obviously thought the game would be relatively easy and fielded a number of his second-line players. Suddenly he realised he had underestimated the Tongans and, early in the second half, brought the whole of his bench on in one hit. They just did the trick and scraped a win.

Of course, everyone knew that the last time England played Tonga in the World Cup in 1999 they had beaten them 101–10. But that was then and this was now. Epi Taione, who has played at centre for Newcastle and Sale, was on the bench for Tonga at Twickenham on that dreadful day. Just before half-time the Tongan prop-forward Ngalu Tauf'on knocked out Richard Hill and was sent off.

Tonga were clearly on their way to a heavy defeat and apparently, at half-time, those on the bench took off their kit, went into the showers and declared they would take no further part in the game. After much shouting with officials they returned to the bench. Taione recalled:

'We were already in the shower but were ordered to get back out there. There were a lot of problems during that World Cup. We were late arriving at the stadium on the morning of the game and we didn't know what the team was … It was a good team but ill-managed. The management were at fault. I think the lessons were learnt after that about the importance of having a good team spirit and getting along as well as players and management.'

Taione and another of the rebellious replacements, scrum-half Sione Tu'ipulotu, would both be playing against England on Friday evening and trying to bring about a very different score-line. Not that it was easy for the Tonga team. Most play professionally outside Tonga but so poor is their rugby federation that the players paid out of their own pockets to return to Tonga so that they could train together. During this World Cup they were being paid less than £50 a week. As Taione says: 'It means a win is sweeter for us than for any other team because we're not doing it for money but for our pride.'

Furthermore, the political situation in Tonga has been very volatile. Last November eight people were killed in anti-monarchy riots and the capital virtually destroyed by fire. Taione again: 'This World Cup is more than just a game of rugby for us. We are trying to bring a smile back to the faces of the Tongan people.'

Mind you, the England team had to worry about whether Prime Minister Gordon Brown – a Scot – was going to call a General Election. As we know, he bottled.

The total population of Tonga is 120,000. The government decreed that everyone should wear red clothing for three days to show support for the rugby team.

Taione concluded:

'England are the world champions and you don't win the World Cup for nothing, so it will take a monumental effort to beat them, but whatever happens we will be happy. I know my people. They are either really good or really bad. There is no warm area with Tonga – just hot or cold. We've done well so far and we're enjoying our rugby. There's no pressure on us now. If there's any pressure, it will be on England.'

– The backs should lie deeper –

That was dead right and everyone in the team and the squad, those in England and those of us in France, knew it. One thing I had noticed, and no doubt many others had too, was that whereas many of the other sides – especially those that were winning their games – seemed to have plenty of space to run and their backs were taking the ball running at nearly full-speed, England's backs seemed to be almost always standing still. In other words, they were lying too flat. Greenwood pointed it out as well:

Many sides – and England all too often – get over-excited when they sniff the line and rush up flat, making it easy for defences to sniff out gilt-edged, try-scoring opportunities. Instead they should sit deeper, giving the three-quarters time to hit the ball at pace.

Ashton picked his team and, though Phil Vickery was available following his two-match suspension for tripping Paul Emerick in the USA game, he put him on the bench and retained Matt Stevens at tight-head prop and Martin Corry as captain.

Whatever Vickery may have felt about this, Stevens certainly felt he deserved to retain his place, saying:

'I'd have been quite angry if I'd not made it. I was prepared for the worst but hoping for the best. It's not easy knowing the England captain is in the same position … You've got to prove that you're better than the captain. But I'd always been told by the coaches that if I did that, I'd be picked no matter what. Fair play, they've made good on their word.'

Perhaps what got Stevens the nod ahead of Vickery was his superior speed around the field, an area where England had been notably poor so far.

Lawrence Dallaglio would be back on the bench. Like Vickery, he would not have happy memories of the game against the USA. Whereas Vickery was cited and given a two-match suspension, Dallaglio had played badly and had been summarily dropped. It could have been the end of his World Cup but, apparently, he fought back in training and Ashton had given him another chance.

There were two changes from the side that beat Samoa. Bath lock Steve Borthwick replaced Simon Shaw and Lewis Moody replaced Joe Worsley who had suffered a slight neck strain. Many were surprised that Mathew Tait was not replaced by the more sturdily built Leicester player, Dan Hipkiss.

England team to face Tonga:
J. Lewsey (Wasps), M. Tait (Newcastle), O. Barkley (Bath), M. Cueto (Sale Sharks), J. Wilkinson (Newcastle), A. Gomarsall (Harlequins), A. Sheridan (Sale Sharks), G. Chuter (Leicester), M. Stevens (Bath), S. Borthwick (Bath), B. Kay (Leicester), M. Corry (Leicester, capt), L. Moody (Leicester), N. Easter (Harlequins).

Replacements:
L. Mears (Bath), P. Vickery (Wasps), L. Dallaglio (Wasps), J. Worsley (Wasps), P. Richards (London Irish), A. Farrell (Saracens), D. Hipkiss (Leicester).

Ashton probably felt the team would need a fully fit strong man to fight against two of Tonga's strongest members, number 8 Fianu Maka and captain Nili Laut.

– Shall we play with green hair? –

As for Tonga, they spent some of the week before the match organising a stunt to repay the Irish betting company Paddy Power, which had sponsored them and enabled them to move to training grounds in New Zealand and England instead of staying at home until the last minute. Our friend Epeli Taione changed his name by deed poll to Paddy Power but the International Rugby Board refused to amend his entry in the tournament guide. The next idea was for the company to send over Irish hairdresser Dermot Hickie, who proceeded to dye the hair of the entire 22-man match squad in various shades of green.

However, the IRB were not going to stand for that ploy either, saying that they could not have the game hijacked by a company that was not an official sponsor. Some of the team were already sporting bright green hairdos, but their management told them they would have to wash it all out.

Back on the field, reappointed captain, Martin Corry was in no doubt about their abilities, saying of their back row:

'Their defensive work is as good as any in the World Cup. In fact, their whole pack of forwards is good. Their line-out drive is solid, their pick-and-go game dangerous. They can turn slow ball into quick ball by going through the guts of you. Tonga are full of confidence and momentum. They're a real threat.'

This game was being played in the old headquarters of French rugby in Paris, the Parc des Princes, and for me it was an emotional return after England's great victory there in the 1999 World Cup. The traditional watering holes at the nearby Porte de St Cloud were the Trois Fontaines and the Trois Obus. Now only the Trois Obus was left, but it seemed as good, friendly and atmospheric as ever.

– A bit of Jonny genius –

Now for the game. England made their intentions clear. Etiquette suggests that the teams are 10 metres apart as Tonga go through their haka. England moved to within 10 inches. However, when the game kicked off, England showed their nerves. Barkley missed a couple of early tackles and Epi Taione broke through an attempted tackle by Jonny Wilkinson to pass to fellow centre Sukanaivalu Hufanga, who forced his way to the try-line. Fortunately relief was at hand when, in the 20th minute, the said Wilkinson spurned an attempt at goal with a kickable penalty and put in a cross-kick for Paul Sackey to chase. He fell as he gathered the ball but the television referee confirmed what we all thought was a fair touch-down. Jonny was definitely back now. It was an inch-perfect, magical kick.

Actually, I think Sackey did incredibly well to keep his eye on the ball because I had the same view as he did and I lost the ball in the glare of the footlights.

If this was supposed to settle England's nerves it was not apparent to us. Fortunately, just before half-time, Sackey was on hand again as he picked up a loose ball in a Tongan attack in England's 22 and sprinted 70 metres to score. I have to say that a real killer of a player would have made sure he got closer to touching down nearer the posts rather than gleefully grinning and flying through the air when he knew he had scored a try. An extra two points might prove vital in what was clearly going to be a close match. Wilkinson duly missed the kick to emphasise the point. Nevertheless, England went in at half-time leading 19–10 and early in the second half moved further ahead. Tait went over for a try following a good break by

Mark Cueto. Wilkinson did not miss the conversion.

England now used their subs, bringing on Phil Vickery, Lawrence Dallaglio and Andy Farrell, the last scoring his first Test try after a dummy loop by Wilkinson. Wilkinson then kicked over his second dropped goal before Tonga scored their second try when their flanker, Pole, squeezed over. The final score was England 36, Tonga 20. So, in spite of all the scares and misfortunes along the way, England had qualified for a quarter-final match against their old World Cup enemy, Australia. Not many people gave them a prayer of winning it, but we would see.

England	Match Data	Tonga
4	Tries	2
2	Conversions	2
2	Penalty goals	2
2	Drop-goals	0
84	Tackles	72
17	Missed tackles	14
79	Carries	69
567	Metres	367
16	Defenders beaten	18
6	Clean breaks	3
8	Offload	10
34	Kicks from hand	26
9	Turnovers conceded	13
9	Penalties conceded	5
0	Yellow cards	0
0	Red cards	0
9	Scrums won	9
12	Line-outs won	11
60	Rucks won	62
51 per cent	Possession	49 per cent
54 per cent	Territory	46 per cent

– 'Slowly improving' –

Brian Ashton's expressed view was:

'It won't do us any harm in the way we have had to fight our way out of the position we were in two weeks ago. We are still not playing to our full potential but we are slowly improving and know we will have to go up another gear against Australia. We are not going to get carried away.'

Paul Ackford's scores for the players moved up another gear from his summaries after the Samoan game and were certainly a long way from the twos and threes he handed out after the South African one.

Sackey even received a nine out of ten and the comment: 'Took first try well and was blisteringly quick for his second.'

I would have deducted two points for his not getting the second try closer to the posts.

He also gave Jonny Wilkinson nine out of ten, saying that he held England together and showed 'great vision' for Sackey's first try.

Gomarsall, Sheridan and Easter all received eights, and the only person to receive less than six was Olly Barkley. He had been very aggressive at the Tongan haka but when it came to what really mattered, the rugby, he missed tackles and an easy drop-goal.

It seemed to me that England had obviously decided to go for territorial position and keeping Tonga as far away as possible from England's 22 by kicking deep on every possible occasion. This may have been wise because Tonga's powerful runners in midfield made Barkley and Tait look very vulnerable. When Farrell replaced Barkley,

Tait began to look more at ease. It was becoming clear that England's forwards were absolutely key to any success they might achieve. It was the one area where they had not disgraced themselves against South Africa.

On we go to a quarter-final tie then, something which seemed a very remote possibility just two weeks ago. For example, Mike Catt was saying to the lads, 'Well done!', in the tone of voice that suggested he did not expect England to go any further.

After the game the Tongans, like the Samoans, assembled for prayers and they too did a lap of honour, and again we all stood and applauded before returning to the Trois Obus to celebrate another victory.

CHAPTER SEVEN

Quarter-final – Australia – Unbelievable!

No one can guarantee success in war, but only deserve it.

Winston Churchill

– 'We all hate England' –

No one was under any illusion as to what the game against Australia would be like. England forward Ben Kay summed it up well when he said:

'Australia have always been the brightest team in world rugby in terms of their intelligence and knowledge of the game. They'll throw something at you that you haven't seen before, do everything well and make the right decisions. We'll have to perform as if our lives depended on it to win.'

Of course, it was Ben Kay who knocked on when the try-line beckoned against Australia in the 2003 final. He would need to forget about that if picked to play on Saturday.

Paul Ackford had turned from, in my view, unnecessarily aggressive criticism to encouragement and even hope, saying that England had given a performance of 'conviction' against Tonga, showing 'accuracy' and 'strength of character', and could prepare to meet Australia 'in the knowledge that they have the makings of an upset'.

Just to keep the pot stirring, John O'Neill, the chief executive of the Australian Rugby Union, announced that 'everyone hates England', saying: 'It doesn't matter whether it's cricket, rugby union, rugby league – we all hate England.'

Challenged as to whether he really meant it or was just trying to wind everyone up, he added:

'I stand by that. Everyone does. All I'm doing is stating the bleeding obvious. If they want further proof, how do they think France won the right to host this World Cup? It is simple. No one would vote for England and they were the only other country in the running. Sadly, this is all a by-product of their born-to-rule mentality. It's been there a long time now and nothing has changed.'

In *The Times*, the excellent journalist Simon Barnes exposed O'Neill's bigotry for what it was and concluded:

I mean born-to-rule mentality, *soooo* last century. These days, Australia is a thrilling cosmopolitan nation with its own style, its own jokes, its own culture … Australia is fabulous, as all English people who visit the place know.

Barnes went on to recall the moment in the 2003 World Cup when an Australian newspaper showed a photograph of Wilkinson kicking and asked: 'Is that all you've got?'

moment England held its breath. With 27 seconds left of the 2003 World Cup final, ...y Wilkinson uses his less-favoured right boot to successfully drop-kick England to a ...7 victory over defending champions Australia at the Telstra Stadium in Sydney.

...s of 2003: Having denied Australia their second consecutive World Cup, England get ... hands on the William Webb Ellis Trophy for the very first time.

Monday, 3 September 2007: England expects. Well, not really, actually. A hug unfancied England side at Heathrow airport turn for a photocall before entering th plane and heading to France to defend their crown.

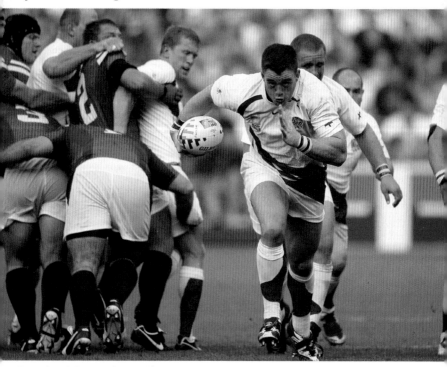

Saturday, 8 September 2007: England open up their campaign against the USA at Sta Felix Bollaert in Lens. English prop Andrew Sheridan makes an early break in a large lacklustre England display.

Having scored England's only try in the 2003 World Cup final, Jason Robinson picked up where he had left off in the tournament, scoring the first try of their 2007 campaign. Nevertheless, it was also the team's first try in their last 176 minutes of international rugby. Here he is tackled by the USA's hard-hitting Paul Emerick, who would later receive a yellow card in the closing minutes of the game for a spear tackle on England's Olly Barkley.

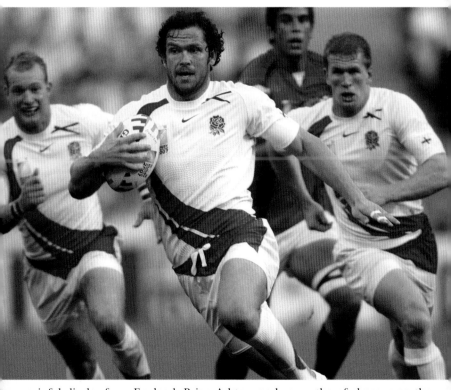

After a painful display from England, Brian Ashton made a swathe of changes on the hour, including Andy Farrell for Mike Catt. Having just conceded a try to the Americans, the England attempt to finish with a flourish, with Farrell making a cutting break through the middle and helping the defending champions limp to a 28–10 win against arguably the worst team in the tournament.

Friday, 14 September 2007: England line up for the national anthem before their Pool match with South Africa at the Stade de France stadium in Saint Denis, outside Paris, venue that would host the same two teams in the final, in a very different game, 36 days la

Playing at fly-half, 36-year-old Mike Catt is dumped by South Africa's 20-year-old cen François Steyn, as England are outclassed in pretty much every department.

Despite a thoroughly commanding performance from South Africa, they stuck to a fairly conservative game plan, with a series of high kicks raining down on full-back Robinson, the only bright spark for England on an otherwise thoroughly miserable night.

Just short of the hour mark, with South Africa 26–0 up, England suffered a hammer blow as their star player embarked on a run in acres of space, only to pull up and hobble to a standstill clutching his left hamstring. He was helped from the field, shirt spattered in blood from a wound above his right eye, before being replaced by Mathew Tait.

gland's players stand dejected as their grip on the Webb Ellis Trophy begins to loosen,
ing down the barrel of a 36–0 thrashing, their first blank scoreline in the history of the
rld Cup.

lay, 21 September 2007: Jonny Wilkinson, yet to play in the tournament due to injury,
s up a kick during a training session at the Beaujoire stadium in Nantes, the venue for
ir win-or-bust pool game with Samoa the following day.

Saturday, 22 September 2007: The hard-hitting Samoans perform the Siva Tau before match as Andrew Sheridan looks on.

England face their second southern hemisphere war-dance in less than a week. To confront Corry and friends with the Kailao before the crucial match at Parc des Prin Paris on Friday, 28 September 2007.

the 76th minute, the England captain bundles over for his second try of the match inst Samoa. Another brace of tries from Wasps' wing Paul Sackey and 24 points from boot of the mercurial Jonny Wilkinson, in a very welcome return, guided England to 4–22 win.

Man of the Match: The marauding Paul Sackey gives England a 19–10 lead as he scores the second of his two first-half tries, his second brace in as many games.

At 19–13, with England's lead having been cut to just six points by a Pierre Hola pen
in the 53rd minute, outside-centre Mathew Tait scored his first try of the tournamer
few minutes later. It proved to be the decisive moment of the match, in that it finally bre
the Tongan resistance and allowed England to play with real rhythm for the first time
their campaign.

Having replaced Olly Barkley at inside-centre after an hour, Andy Farrell scores his first international try following a dummy loop move with Wilkinson and a dart for the line. Wilkinson converted the score to make it 33–13 and put the game out of Tonga's reach. Wilkinson added a further drop-goal, and although Tonga scored a try in the dying throes of the game, England had secured a 36–20 win and booked themselves a place in the last eight.

Shortly after the final whistle with Tonga, Wilkinson's thoughts immediately move on to the quarter-final showdown with Australia the following weekend.

Saturday, 10 October 2007: England line up for the national anthem before their quar[ter] final clash with Australia at the Vélodrome stadium in Marseille, Bouches-du-Rhô[ne]. Australia had waltzed through their group to the knockout stage with a positive points [dif]ference of 174. No one gave England a prayer.

On 14 minutes, a lovely delayed pass from England lock Simon Shaw (not shown) p[ut] Jason Robinson into space in midfield, only to be stopped by a great tackle fr[om] Australian scrum-half George Gregan. England's win brought an end to a stellar [Test] career for Gregan, who retired after the game with 139 international caps, a runners[-up] medal from 2003 and a winner's medal from 1999.

dbags at 4pm. Props Andrew Sheridan and Matt Dunning lock horns after a scrum
in the second half. Sheridan, 'Big Ted' or 'The Beast of Bromley', went on to be
ed Man of the Match for a searing forward display in which he wrecked Australia's
m and made hard yards in the loose.

and pretty much dominated the scrum throughout the match, winning two against
ead. Nevertheless, some good early work by the England pack was undone with some
discipline at the breakdown.

With England's scrum having destroyed Australia's yet again, the Wallabies concede[d] penalty in the 60th minute as flanker Rocky Elsom tried to get the ball from Nick Eas[t's] grasp at the base. Here Jonny Wilkinson strikes his fourth penalty to put England 12 ahead. His tally of 12 points in the game made him the top points-scorer in the histor[y] the World Cup, taking him seven points past former Scotland full-back Gavin Hastings'

England's Martin Corry celebrates as the referee blows for full-time. Australia's Stir[ling] Mortlock had narrowly missed a difficult penalty kick from 45 metres out in the 7[?] minute, which would have won the Wallabies the match. Instead, England held on to t[heir] 12–10 lead, securing a semi-final spot that few would have thought believable at the s[tart] of the campaign.

As dejected Australians try to come to terms with another World Cup defeat at the hands of England, the English struggle to contain their joy.

It went OK, didn't it? Lawrence Dallaglio sums up the nation's thoughts.

Saturday, 13 October 2007: Fans begin to gather near the Eiffel Tower during the day ah of the evening's semi-final clash between England and France at the Stade de France.

England enjoy a dream start as Andy Gomarsall's kick into the corner is gathered by Lewsey, who proceeds to bundle over France's full-back Damien Traille for a try in second minute of the match.

up within 78 seconds, and the hordes of English fans erupt with joy.

k Regan makes a break, ably supported by Simon Shaw, who had another stunning game.

Prop Phil Vickery finds himself temporarily acting as scrum-half. The England captain his socks off until he finally ran out of steam and was replaced by Matt Stevens wit minutes to go.

France's Sébastien 'Caveman' Chabal charges past England's Andy Gomarsall and Ge Chuter late in the game. Chabal, who had started on the bench, had been require early as the 25th minute when veteran lock Fabien Pelous had been forced off after a s ing tackle by Jonny Wilkinson.

and were awarded a penalty in the 75th minute following a high tackle on Jason
Inson by replacement hooker Dimitri Szarzewski. Jonny Wilkinson subsequently slots
second successful penalty of the night to take the score to 11–9 and give England the
for the first time since the 18th minute.

he dying minutes of the match, the English pack successfully engineered rolling maul
r rolling maul through the French half. Jonny Wilkinson lurked with intent through-
The second the maul collapsed, the ball was fired back to the fly-half. He made no
ake with the drop goal: 14–9. England led by five points with two minutes to go …

The England players celebrate as the final whistle goes. Against all the odds, they reached their second consecutive World Cup final.

Having just earned his 50th cap, Jason Robinson celebrates securing the opportunit bow out of the game on the grandest stage of all.

Vickery blows a kiss to the noisy English fans who had remained in the Stade de ↲ce to celebrate their side's semi-final win well after the final whistle.

Friday, 19 October 2007: The day before the final. Jonny Wilkinson arrives at the Stade
France for a practice session.

Saturday, 20 October 2007: English and South African fans gather near the Eiffel To
ahead of the evening's World Cup final. Over 50,000 England supporters – many with
tickets – made the trip to Paris with the hope of getting themselves one of the prized
of paper which were said to be changing hands for in excess of £1,500.

nce Harry holds a piece of string in his mouth as he attaches an England flag to rail-
s in the Stade de France prior to kick-off.

me on lads! From left to right: England's Martin Corry, Mathew Tait, Jonny Wilkinson,
ke Catt, Nick Easter, Andy Gomarsall and Lewis Moody line up for the national
hems. Although owner of a winner's medal from 2003, at 36 years old, Catt knows this
be his last World Cup final.

South African prop C.J. van der Linde gives 6ft 9in, 19-stone Simon Shaw the treatm
as he bundles him over the top of team-mate Schalk Burger.

England begin the second half sensationally as Mathew Tait tears a whole through
middle of the South African defence, beating four men with a series of side-steps a
swerves before being stopped just short of the line.

wing Tait's superb run, England recycled the ball to the left, where Jonny Wilkinson
ded to Mark Cueto for a fantastic try right in the corner.

ngland celebrate, Irish referee Alain Rolland and French touch judge Joel Jutge look to
another before turning to the Australian video official Stuart Dickinson for confirma-
After three agonising minutes of deliberation, Cueto was ruled to have been in touch
he made the score and the try was disallowed. It was a crushing moment for England.

Advantage had been played in the lead-up to the disallowed try by the referee from an
lier offence by South Africa's Schalk Burger and so he awarded England a penalty. Jo
Wilkinson duly secures the three points – albeit off the post – alleviating some of the
of the disallowed try and pulling England's deficit back to 9–6.

fway through the second half, Toby Flood – who had replaced Mike Catt shortly before
st fails to latch on to Andy Gomarsall's chip into the corner and gives the covering
cy Montgomery a little shove in the back which sends the full-back flying over the
ertising hoardings and into a TV camera. South Africa weren't too impressed with
od, but the referee let the Englishman off with a warning.

ly Whizz' is tackled by South African players Bakkies Botha and Fourie du Preez.
binson would later have to hobble from the field with an injury that brought a glitter-
career to a close. He received a standing ovation, and even in the intensity of a World
p final, South Africa's Bryan Habana made sure that he tapped Robinson's hand as a
w of respect as he left the field.

George Chuter – a replacement for Mark Regan in the second half – is caught by So[...]
Africa's Man of the Match Victor Matfield as Ben Kay arrives in support.

...ces William and Harry and friends – like the rest of the nation – show their appreci-
...n of a battling England performance.

...th Africa's scrum-half Fourie du Preez fires the ball out to his fly-half late in the sec-
...half. England did a good job of subduing du Preez in the final after he had been so
...rumental in the pool match five weeks before.

Huge man, huge heart, huge work-rate. It takes both François Steyn and Schalk Burge
try to bring Simon Shaw – arguably England's player of the tournament – to a halt.

th Africa celebrate as the final whistle goes. With the final score at 15–9, they had
ome World Champions for the second time.

France 2007

England players contemplate what could have been as they collect their runners-up
als.

South Africa's captain John Smit is presented with the William Webb Ellis Trophy French President Nicolas Sarkozy and South African President Thabo Mbeki.

The England coach speaks for the nation: Brian Ashton tells his players that they ca proud of what they had achieved over the last six weeks – a sentiment not lost on any back home.

The *Daily Mirror* responded with a picture of Kylie Minogue's bum and exactly the same words: 'Is that all *you've* [in red] got?'

Australian winger Lote Tuqiri also voiced criticism of the England team: 'I don't like to say it but Jason [Robinson] is probably their only world-class back, and the only one playing in form.'

Injured Australian captain Stirling Mortlock could not resist adding his bit: 'You grow up wanting to beat England. By the time you're an adult, you feel like it's the most important thing in the world.'

It was probably true but it didn't half set up Australia for ridicule if by any chance they lost to this hated, haughty, nearly useless team. In any case, although they don't seem able to resist it, the Australians should realise that such comments, far from unsettling opponents, tend to bind them closer together. It's a bit like brothers constantly squabbling but as soon as an outsider criticises one of them, they become best mates: 'Hang on, that's my brother you're talking about. Watch it!'

– The lovely Marseille –

The action had now moved to Marseille, a compact town surrounded by mountains and the sea. (That's why the town did not suffer the racial problems other big French cities did in 2006. Marseille had to absorb their immigrants – they couldn't shove them off into ghettoes.)

Marseille is a town with a big history. It is certain that human beings have inhabited the town and its environs for nearly 30,000 years because Palaeolithic cave paintings in the underwater Cosquer cave near the Calanque of Morgiou date back to between 27,000 and 19,000 BC. Modern Marseille was founded in 600 BC by Greeks from Phocaea who used it as a trading port.

They called it Massalia and ran it successfully until it was absorbed into the Roman Empire, in which it continued to thrive as a port. As the Roman Empire declined the town reverted to the Franks, and the name Marseille was adopted. After various travails including severe attacks of bubonic plague, Marseille became, in the 15th century, France's most fortified town apart from Paris – and indeed, it soon acquired a reputation for rebelling against central government. By the time Louis XIV came to the throne he was forced to march on the town to quell an uprising against the governor. As a result, the two forts of St Jean and St Nicolas, which still guard the city today, were erected above the harbour and a fleet was established in the harbour itself. During the 18th century Marseille became France's leading military port in the Mediterranean.

At the end of the century the local population joined the Revolution with gusto and sent 500 volunteers to Paris in 1792 to help defend the revolutionary government. While marching they sang what became the national anthem of France, the rousing 'Marseillaise'. During the 19th century Marseille continued to flourish both as an industrial centre and as a port, by this time servicing the French colonies in Africa, notably Algeria.

On into the 20th century, and the city suffered from bombing by both the German and Italian air forces before being occupied by the Germans, who destroyed much of the old quarter in an effort to stamp out resistance. Much of the city was rebuilt in the 1950s with the help of reparation payments from Germany and Italy. In the late 1950s and early 1960s there was a massive inflow of immigrants, mainly from Algeria, and this has given Marseille a vibrant French-African atmosphere. In May 2006, the French financial magazine *L'Expansion* named Marseille the most dynamic of France's large cities, showing that no fewer than 7,200 companies had been founded since 2000.

There were plenty of places for the rugby tourists to visit as they waited for the next big clash of their teams:

• The Old Port or Vieux-Port, the main harbour and marina of the city is one of the main places to eat in the city. Dozens of cafés line the waterfront. The Quai des Belges at the end of the harbour is the site of the daily fish market. Much of the northern quayside area was rebuilt by the architect Fernand Pouillon after its destruction by the Nazis in 1943.

• The Phare de Sainte Marie, a lighthouse on the inlet to the Old Port.

• La Vieille Charité in the Panier, an architecturally significant building designed by the Puget brothers. The central baroque chapel is situated in a courtyard lined with arcaded galleries. Originally built as an alms house, it is now home to an archaeological museum and a gallery of African and Asian art, as well as bookshops and a café.

• The Centre Bourse and the adjacent rue St Ferreol district (including rue du Rome and rue Paradis), the main shopping area in central Marseille. (The other two major shopping complexes in Marseille are at la Valentine and le Grand Littoral.)

• The Musée d'Histoire, the Marseille historical museum, located in the Centre Bourse. It contains records of the Greek and Roman history of Marseille as well as the best-preserved hull of a 6th-century boat in the world. Ancient remains from the Hellenic port are displayed in the adjacent archaeological gardens, the Jardin des Vestiges.

• The Palais de la Bourse, a 19th-century building housing the chamber of commerce, the first such institution in France. It also contains a small museum, charting the maritime and commercial history of Marseille, as well as a separate collection of models of ships.

On the sporting front, the city's football club, Olympique de Marseille, play at the impressive Stade Vélodrome, and that is where the games in the 2007 World Cup are being played. Olympique de Marseille have enjoyed great success, winning the UEFA Cup in 1999 and 2004. Unfortunately, they were tainted somewhat by the match-fixing scandals in the 1990s of the then owner, Bernard Tapie.

In this compact area the England team could get close to their supporters, of whom there were many thousand. Martin Corry, shrugging off the Australian criticism, said:

'By the time the weekend comes around there will also be thousands of Englishmen on hand to cheer our every move. The centre of Marseille around the Vieux-Port is much more compact than Paris and by kick-off it will feel just like a home fixture.'

Former Springbok player Nick Mallett, writing in the *Daily Telegraph*, was in little doubt that England would lose, saying:

I would like to be more positive about England, I would like to trot out a few misty-eyed lines from the romantic poets, but modern rugby is just not that wistful – and the pragmatic Aussies very, very rarely lose to England when they have the better team. The Aussie coach John Connolly has made all sorts of tactful noises about how he would have preferred a quarter-final against South Africa, but he is talking absolute horse manure. He is delighted to be playing England.

The only area where England have an obvious advantage is in the scrum. Andrew Sheridan will be relishing the opportunity to take Aussie props apart as he has once before. But Connolly is a very good forwards coach and he will have his pack too well organised for that to happen. Where the game will be won (by Australia) and lost (by England) is in the back row and the three-quarters. England just do not have a ball carrying forward like Rocky Elsom, who gives the Aussies so much momentum going forward.

Nor do they have the sort of midfield power and precision that Australia have in Matt Giteau and Stirling Mortlock. The likes of Mathew Tait and Jason Robinson may be able to do something with a broken field, but they are not line-breakers like Mortlock. England have a lot of hard-working, honest club players, but that is not usually enough to take a team to the semi-final of a World Cup. You suspect that St Jonny will have to perform a miracle but, good though he was against Tonga, this match will surely prove beyond him.

Mallett also predicted that New Zealand would beat France by 20 points and had a go at the organisers for putting three of the six best sides in the world in the same pool so that the home side were now playing in the quarter-final in Wales instead of at home. Ah yes, Nick, but who would have thought France would lose to Argentina in the opening game?

– 'I've always rated England' –

On the Wednesday before Saturday's game, Australian coach John Connolly decided that praise for England rather than patronising criticism might work better and might induce a sense of complacency in the England team. He told people:

'I've always rated England as a huge threat to Australia, because we mirror each other in some ways in terms of the line-outs and how we play a little bit. One-off games make every one very nervous because you're playing for so much.

'Sheridan is just a wonderful athlete. He's plotted a path since his Bristol days five years ago from lock to the front row to that demolition of Australia in 2005, he gained a huge reputation out of that. He's one of the better props in world rugby, not only in scrummaging but around the field.

'England have all the gears to provide a huge threat to anyone. They have a better driving maul than most countries in the world. I know what emphasis they put on it after being there for quite a while.'

That day, Brian Ashton picked his team and replacements:

Team: J. Robinson (unattached), P. Sackey (Wasps), M. Tait (Newcastle), A. Farrell (Saracens), J. Lewsey (Wasps), J. Wilkinson (Newcastle), A. Gomarsall (Harlequins), A. Sheridan (Sale Sharks), M. Regan (Bristol), P. Vickery (Wasps, capt), S. Shaw (Wasps), B. Kay (Leicester), M. Corry (Leicester), L. Moody (Leicester), N. Easter (Harlequins).

Replacements: G. Chuter (Leicester), M. Stevens (Bath), L. Dallaglio (Wasps), J. Worsley (Wasps), P. Richards (London Irish), O. Barkley (Bath), D. Hipkiss (Leicester).

There were five changes from the starting line-up against Tonga. Andy Farrell replaced Olly Barkley, and Phil Vickery replaced Matt Stevens and also took over the captaincy again. Mark Regan replaced George Chuter and Simon Shaw replaced Steve Borthwick. All those replaced would start on the bench except Borthwick, who missed out on the 22 altogether.

The return of Jason Robinson was a near-miracle. We had all thought that when he limped off in the South Africa game that was the end of his career. He was picked at full-back and Josh Lewsey moved to the wing, replacing Mark Cueto. Paul Sackey seemed very secure now after his poor performance against South Africa where he had been put on the right wing instead of his usual place on the left. And, of course, he had picked up two tries in each of the Samoa and Tonga games.

Not everyone was happy with some of the selections. For example, former England forward Brian Moore wondered whether Jason Robinson was fully fit and thought that he should be on the wing with Lewsey at full-back. He also thought that Dan Hipkiss should have been chosen ahead of Andy Farrell and finally, that Matt Stevens should have started instead of Phil Vickery. He predicted that England would lose.

Brian Ashton was having none of the criticism levelled at him for selecting Farrell, saying:

'We felt we needed a direct approach for this game. For the threat Andy brings to the opposition line, for his kicking game, his defensive work, his general leadership and game management, we felt this was what we were looking for on Saturday. It may have taken Andy a while to get to the level he is at now, but he's looked sharper and sharper as the tournament has gone on.'

How much ball Farrell would receive remained a moot point. We could all see that Ashton felt, almost certainly correctly, that it would be a massive battle up-front, and accordingly he had picked his most experienced front five.

In the event, and continuing England's bad luck with injuries, Farrell was forced to withdraw on the Thursday when he strained a calf muscle. Ashton decided to delay the choice of his replacement until the next day. It would seem to be a straight choice between Olly Barkley and Mike Catt, although some might favour Toby Flood or Dan Hipkiss, but Barkley was now doubtful because he had suffered a dead leg in the same session that Farrell strained his calf muscle.

– Will Regan 'behave himself'? –

Meanwhile, and in contravention of instructions from the International Rugby Board, Australian coach John Connolly made public the fact that he had spoken to the IRB referees manager, Paddy O'Brien, and asked him to ensure that England hooker Mark Regan 'behaves himself', as he put it. When asked about this move, Connolly said: 'England picking Regan at hooker delivers an intent. We've spoken to Paddy O'Brien to ensure he behaves himself. Just to ensure the game's fair, clean.'

Of course, Connolly used to coach Regan at Bath, so he

could tell O'Brien that he knew Regan of old. Olly Barkley responded with: 'That's knuckles [Connolly] for you. He's up to his usual pre-match PR tricks.'

Australian number 8 Wycliff Palu followed this up by saying he expected 'plenty of niggle' from the England pack, adding:

'The team that controls their discipline will get over the top. You've just got to control yourself and get them back some other way – a big tackle or something. If you give away a silly penalty, especially with Jonny Wilkinson playing, you give away three points.'

When Friday came, Ashton picked the experienced Mike Catt to replace Farrell. It would be his 73rd cap for England and his 12th against Australia. Almost unbelievably, he had not played with Wilkinson for four years.

He said, on hearing of his selection:

'A lot of things have happened in the past four years, so we will just see how the game progresses. We need to work as a pairing in terms of our decision-making.

'All of us realise that things went wrong in the South Africa game. We had a chat about it on the Saturday and Sunday afterwards, we corrected it and things went a lot better against Samoa and Tonga.

'We just didn't have any structure in our game. South Africa were very good in how they stuck to a game plan, whereas with us the understanding wasn't there.

'But that was three weeks ago, and a lot of water has passed under the bridge. There has been a lot of discussions since then, and we seem to be back on track and going in the right direction.

'Whether we have gone as far as we want to be, I am not really sure. We are going in the right direction, but we are underdogs.'

The Wallabies' team was:

Australia: Chris Latham, Adam Ashley-Cooper, Stirling Mortlock (capt), Matt Giteau, Lote Tuqiri, Berrick Barnes, George Gregan, Wycliff Palu, George Smith, Rocky Elsom, Dan Vickerman, Nathan Sharpe, Guy Shepherdson, Stephen Moore, Matt Dunning.

Replacements: Adam Freier, Al Baxter, Hugh McMeniman, Stephen Hoiles, Phil Waugh, Julian Huxley, Drew Mitchell.

– 'Australia will score tries today' –

Just to give England encouragement on the day before their quarter-final against Australia, *The Times* published a survey showing that 51 per cent of the 1,000 people questioned said that Andy Robinson was to blame for England's 'lifeless showing'. The opening paragraph of the article read:

The post mortem into England's World Cup may soon be in full swing, even if the chances of England making it past the quarter-finals are now slightly better than Tony Blair being included in the next Cabinet reshuffle.

And *The Guardian* added its bit by quoting Ladbrokes' David Williams as saying: 'Punters have all but given up on the northern hemisphere teams. The southern hemisphere teams seem to be playing on a different level.' Australia were 4–1 on to beat England.

On the morning of the match, Shaun Edwards wrote in

The Guardian: 'Australia will score tries today.'

On the day itself, *The Independent*'s Chris Hewett tried to figure out ways that England could win, but was forced to conclude: 'The likelihood must be that the Webb Ellis Trophy will be out of English hands by tea-time.'

On the other hand, England's Martin Corry, also writing in *The Guardian*, found some hope:

Sometimes you go into games with a gut feeling. Without wishing to tempt fate, I've been convinced all week that our match with Australia will not be settled until the last 10 minutes. We're the underdogs and we're aware we have to improve substantially. But if it comes down to a streetfight we know how to handle ourselves. Our goal is to ensure we're still in contention at the 70-minute mark.

If we can do so we'll have a chance, regardless of previous form in this tournament.

We were nervous, partly because victories over Samoa and Tonga had given us some hope, whereas after the South African game our attitude had been one of despair: the rugby's hopeless but let's enjoy France while we're here. Now, we knew it was a long shot, but there was a sneaking hope that we might somehow overcome the Wallabies. Common sense and the experience of the last few weeks – and perhaps the last two years – told us we were going to lose, possibly get hammered, but there was just that little hope and that made you nervous because you did not want to be disappointed. But think of the strength of the Wallabies, the only side that had beaten the All Blacks in 2007. All the so-called experts were saying that we hadn't a cat-in-hell's chance.

Perceptively, Will Greenwood identified the scrum as one place where the Australians might be vulnerable. Ashton's selections suggested that he had worked that out as well. It still left us worrying about Matt Giteau and Stirling Mortlock. Would Catt and Tait be able to stop them? Wilkinson should be a match for Australian fly-half Berrick Barnes, substituting for the injured Steve Larkham, but the youngster had already shown that he was no slouch. Indeed, he was almost certainly a world-class player in the making.

The four previous encounters in the World Cup between the two sides had ended in two wins for Australia and two for England. In far-off 1987 in a pool match, Australia had won 19–6 in a relatively easy victory. In the 1991 final at Twickenham, Australia won again 12–6 and could probably congratulate themselves on goading England into playing expansively instead of sticking to the tight game that had served them so well up to that point. In 1995 in South Africa it was England's turn just to win a very close contest 25–22 as Rob Andrew kicked a late drop-goal. And then the famous final in 2003 when, again, a drop-goal in extra time by Jonny Wilkinson took England to a 20–17 victory. Two all, then.

We came down to the Stade Vélodrome by coach from Aix-en-Provence where we were staying. The previous day we had gone into the spectacular Vieux-Port which was crammed with yachts of every shape and size. In the key berth in the very centre was the biggest of the lot and it was sporting a Welsh flag – at half-mast. What a shame! As Englishmen we really felt for the Welsh not making the quarter-final. Mind you, their game against Fiji was the game of the tournament so far.

There were lots of confident Australians around but at least they were not arrogant like many of the South Africans. Nevertheless, we were gradually realising that we were still in this tournament, and who knew what might happen?

– Who was collapsing the scrum? –

England started well but were perhaps over-eager and conceded four penalties in the first 20 minutes.

In fact, by my calculation, at that point I don't think England had been awarded either a penalty or even a scrum.

Others around me were starting to liken it to the refereeing in the final in Sydney in 2003. They reckoned that this referee penalised England for handling the ball when the Australian forwards had simply dropped the ball. In the set scrums the Wallaby forward Matt Dunning couldn't hack it, collapsing in five of the first six scrums, and Guy Shepherdson was obviously already struggling to cope with Andrew Sheridan. In spite of this, the referee awarded the first two scrum penalties against England. As Vickery said later, 'this was "very strange" and you have to ask yourself the question – if England were pushing Australia, as they were, why would they deliberately collapse the scrum?'

When we had been fearing for our lives before this game, should we not have remembered the England 26–16 victory over the Wallabies in November 2005 when Sheridan had completely dominated the scrum? Al Baxter couldn't cope and was eventually sent to the sin bin for constantly collapsing the scrum. Matt Dunning had tried to take on Sheridan instead and was carried off on a stretcher. The Wallabies then asked for – and got – uncontested scrums. Why had we forgotten that?

Anyway, we were reminded of it now, and a lovely experience it was too.

Fortunately, only one of the penalties had been converted and so England were only 3–0 down. And England attacking play through Wilkinson and Catt was looking better than anything we had seen so far. Then England were, at last, awarded some penalties and Wilkinson scored twice. But in the last ten minutes of the first half Australia's backs finally got going, and in the end the constant pressure told and Tuqiri went over for a try, as he had in the 2003 final. Mortlock converted and England were 10–6 down. We feared the worst.

Our fears were heightened by Wilkinson missing – for him – two relatively easy penalties, but then he did score one and the gap was just one point. At the very least it looked certain we would not be humiliated, and I guess it was a measure of our state of mind that that was such a relief. Ye Gods, even better, England went into the lead in the 60th minute when Wilkinson kicked another penalty to make it 12–10. Twenty minutes to go – an eternity!

– Swing low, sweet chariot –

England now brought on their substitutes. Toby Flood came on for Catt, Matt Stevens for Vickery and Joe Worsley for Moody. They hung in there but then, horror of horrors, conceded a kickable penalty in the dying moments. Would Stirling Mortlock dash the possible cry of triumph from our lips? We could not watch but we had to. He missed! We had won! We could hardly believe it, but by God did we sing 'Swing low, sweet chariot' with gusto as the team made their lap of honour.

Wilkinson had kicked all the points to become the highest points-scorer in World Cup history. He would grab the headlines, but in truth it was the forwards 'wot won it'. Andrew Sheridan and Phil Vickery were outstanding. And if Mortlock had succeeded with that final kick, Wilkinson would have been ruing his three attempts at goal that missed.

Ashton was, quite rightly, ecstatic. If this was a book on the other type of football I would be tempted to write that he was 'over the moon'. Everyone wanted to hear what he had to say. This is some of what he did say:

'I think today you saw a group of players who showed a lot of physical courage and also the other kind of courage. Physical courage is a given at international level but I thought we showed a lot of the other type in the first 20 to 25 minutes by taking Australia on in a way that I suspect most people expected Australia to take us on – by moving the ball around the field and challenging in all sorts of different areas ... To say it was magnificent is probably an understatement but I can't think of a better word at the moment.'

England had not scored any tries, but they came close when a very fast pass from Wilkinson bounced off Mike Catt's chest – he would almost certainly have scored had he caught it.

What did Paul Ackford think of it all? Now the superlatives were really to the fore, with Andrew Sheridan receiving a full ten out of ten. Simon Shaw received nine with the comment: 'Another excellent effort. Great hands, great attitude and a big lump in the collisions.' As for Andy Gomarsall, he also got nine and the comment: 'Comprehensively out-played George Gregan.' Not many people have done that, and indeed Will Greenwood had marked Gregan out as Australia's real danger man.

And, of course, the English Sundays went mad: WINNING POMS in the *Sunday Times*; MAGNIFIQUE (reflecting France's equally unexpected victory over New Zealand in the evening after England's win – we haven't come to that yet) in *The Observer*; JONNY'S ON TOP OF THE WORLD in the *Mail on Sunday*; and MAGNIFICENT ENGLAND in the *Sunday Telegraph*. It was all so different from the headlines of just three weeks earlier.

Stuart Barnes wrote in the *Sunday Times* that 'Forward dominance and intelligent play proved to be a heady mix for England'.

It proved to be a heady mix for us in the Stade Vélodrome as well. What had seemed a rather over-whelming and forbidding place suddenly became like a festival of light. Weeks of suffering turned into moments of delight. How had those forwards who had seemed so slow and witless turned into the tyros that knocked the Wallabies' scrum backwards? We had been told to fear the free-running and skilful Australian backs. In the event, they had about three or four dangerous runs.

– 'Cheats and conmen' –

After the comments of some of the Australian manage-ment and team before the match, this victory was one to savour. And Stephen Jones of the *Sunday Times* did not pull any punches when he wrote what he thought of the Australian forwards:

There was another reason to be pleased at this glory from nowhere. It means that Australia were dumped. Good rid-dance. They have some marvellous pedigree players, it was sad to see George Gregan, dominated by Andy Gomarsall, go out on a low. But especially up front, Australia were a bunch of cheap-shop cheats and conmen and for long periods of the match the referee let them collapse, cheat and recoil from the weight. They tried to punch Sheridan into submission, Sheridan briefly felt his jaw a few times, and he and the rejuvenated Phil Vickery went back to smashing them.

Some of the England players were overcome emotionally after the game. Andy Gomarsall was in tears but managed to say:

'The spirit in the squad was incredible, just phenomenal. It wasn't pretty, a bit like my face, and I can't believe it, to be honest. It was sheer grit and bloody-mindedness. I was emotional before the game and after. You have to treasure the opportunities of beating sides like Australia.'

And Gomarsall and Wilkinson both sang the praises of Simon Shaw, saying how incredible he was. Shaw himself must have been delighted after so many setbacks and disappointments in his career. I was not so sure about Shaw's performance. He dropped some passes and was also penalised, whether fairly or not, a couple of times.

For the Australians, coach John Connolly – who was retiring from his position, as were George Gregan and Steve Larkham – said:

'We never got momentum. England dismantled our breakdown and we lost our composure. England's scrum was world-class and I've said all along that and having Wilkinson makes them very dangerous.'

Mark Regan, who, of course, had been singled out as an aggressive troublemaker before the game by John Connolly, reckoned the turning point of the game was when 'they had a scrum which we made a mess of, kicked hurriedly to touch on their own line, making only a few yards, and then collapsed our maul following a lineout take. It was the key moment in the game.' Collapsing the maul gave England a penalty which Wilkinson converted, taking the score to 10–9. I knew we had them, said Regan.

– 'The north lives' –

While England were quietly, and for some not so quietly, celebrating, the most amazing thing was happening in the Millennium Stadium in Cardiff where, somewhat bizarrely, France were playing New Zealand.

The All Blacks always had been, and still were, odds-on favourites to win this World Cup. But then, they always are. And they started against France – who had shocked everyone by losing to Argentina in the opening match, thereby risking elimination before the knock-out stage – as though they were favourites and this game was just a stepping stone on the way to their ultimate triumph. There was a lot of kicking backwards and forwards in the first half before the All Blacks began to dominate. They went in at half-time leading 13–3 and we feared for France in the second half. However, France did not fear for themselves. A penalty after McAllister received a yellow card for impeding Yannick Jauzion made it 13–6. Perhaps the All Blacks were not so sure of themselves after all. Was it a sign of desperation that Dan Carter tried a drop-goal from the half-way line?

France changed their kicking game into a running game and scored a try that meant 13–13 when it was converted. Then came what, in retrospect, was a seminal moment. The talismanic All Blacks fly-half, Dan Carter, limped off. Nevertheless, New Zealand scored another try: 18–13. But France were not finished. A superb break by Freddie Michalak – who else? – put Jauzion through to score a try. The conversion made it 20–18 and somehow France held on for another famous – and unexpected – victory.

L'Equipe, the French sports paper, went wild on the day after France beat the All Blacks. Under the headline C'EST IMMENSE, it shouted: 'L'equipe de France a réalisé, hier soir à Cardiff, une des plus grandes performances de son histoire en battant les All Blacks.'

The rugby supplement simply said: TELLEMENT FRANÇAIS. And then under the heading, 'L'essai de la révolte': 'À la 54 minute, les Français marquèrent un essai qui changea le cours de l'histoire récit.'

The loquacious old veteran, Eddie Butler, could hardly believe it. He wrote in *The Observer*:

Oh my sweet rugby goodness. The north lives. What a day in the Rugby World Cup. What a day in rugby. What a day in sport … All around me here in Toulouse the car horns are going off … Bonkers is cool … For a day or two we should just celebrate the fact that the northern hemisphere has rediscovered its soul on the most dramatic day in rugby I have ever known.

What was the reaction down under? The Australian press were reasonably restrained:

The Australian: 'Australia's World Cup dream is over, throttled at the hands of a massive England pack that simply scrummed the Wallabies into the turf. As referee Alain Rolland signalled full time, the Wallabies stood stunned and still, massive favourites brought low by a limited but well drilled and extremely committed English side.'

The Sunday Herald Sun: 'Wallabies booted from World Cup by England.'

Sydney Morning Herald: 'You've got to be choking, it's a new world order.'

The Sunday Times (Perth): 'England were written off as one-dimensional, a band of ageing veterans. But their Grumpy Old Men were having none of it as their forwards ran rampant.'

– 'A bunch of boofheads' –

In New Zealand, the rugby commentator Murray Dexter said:

Sadly, we are a dumb rugby nation; we don't play the big matches well. We were a bunch of boofheads playing out there tonight against a French side that isn't that good. On the big occasions we choke.

And the New Zealanders themselves did not take kindly to the defeat. A lot of flak was aimed at referee Wayne Barnes. The Chairman of the New Zealand Union, Jock Hobbs, said: 'Some of the decisions the referee made had an enormous bearing on the outcome. In our view some of the decisions were very, very questionable.'

The New Zealanders did not like the sin-binning of Luke McAllister and they were incensed by the missing of what they saw as a forward pass when Yannick Jauzion scored his match-winning try. Barnes became the subject of a barrage of abuse on internet sites and was branded New Zealand's 'most wanted man'.

Paddy O'Brien, a former international referee and a New Zealander himself and now manager of the tournament's match officials, defended Barnes as a 'super referee' and said: 'The pass was forward but that's rugby refereeing. Sport is about winning and losing and New

Zealand lost, let's get on with life.'

The *New Zealand Herald*'s headline said it all: 'DÉJÀ VU ALL OVER AGAIN … AND AGAIN … AND AGAIN.'

New Zealand Foreign Minister Winston Peters felt that the ramifications of the defeat would spread wide, saying:

'It would have been a big lift for our country psychologically and a big lift economically as well. When people feel better, they produce more, they work harder, they are just happier. They don't beat up their children and their wives – so you know it's a tragedy.'

Of course, the Aussies consoled themselves a bit by crowing about the New Zealanders. The *Sydney Herald* wrote: 'At least the Kiwis got stuffed too.'

And I'm afraid some northern journalists did not hold back either. Brendan Gallagher really went for the All Blacks' attitude in an article in the *Daily Telegraph* under the headline ALL BLACKS CHOKE ON ARROGANCE, and concluded with a summary of their defeats from 1991 onwards:

1991: Semi-final, Dublin, L 16–6
Aged team done in cold blood by Australia. David Campese's finest moment, with Tim Horan not far behind.

1995: Final, Johannesburg, L 15–12
Looked superb going into the final but failed to fire against a Nelson Mandela-inspired South Africa. Then tried to blame a hotel waitress for poisoning them.

1999: Semi-final, London, L 43–31
Relied too heavily on Jonah Lomu to build a lead and were then blitzed by an inspired France in an epic at Twickenham.

2003: Semi-final, Sydney, L 22–10
Stroppy and unapproachable for most of the tournament, New Zealand went into their shells and played like drains against Australia.

2007: Quarter-final, Cardiff, L 20–18
Froze against a clever but hardly vintage French side. Big names failed to deliver, little leadership and tactically inept.

As for us, we went off for dinner after the game. It was going to be a long evening, because kick-off had been three o'clock in the afternoon. I expected we would cope. And then, of course, there was the France vs. New Zealand match which we watched on a big screen. Needless to say, the French supporters groaned a bit in the first half and then gradually became more and more excited as their team came back at the All Blacks. When they eventually won, the French around us went bananas and no doubt carried on doing so through the night. We had to catch the last coach back to Aix-en-Provence but, of course, the party was in full swing there too. Our hotel was in the student quarter and I was prevailed on to sing our national anthem after they had given many renditions of the 'Marseillaise'. *L'Entente cordiale* was in good shape that night. I noted that I'd better wash my now rather dirty and smelly T-shirt so that I could carry on wearing it. It had really served its purpose because it reminded Australia of our great 2003 victory. On the front was a big English rose with the words 'World Cup Winners 2003' underneath. On the back the results of all the seven games we played.

Having suffered from heavy defeats by the All Blacks and also having had to listen to them portrayed as out-and-out favourites for the 2007 World Cup for the previous four years, there were plenty of people ready to enjoy their humiliation. Also it must be said – for those still in the competition – there was almost certainly relief that France had managed to get rid of them.

Furthermore, most of us could remember the horrendous spear tackle on Lions captain Brian O'Driscoll in the first few minutes of the first Test on the last Lions tour to New Zealand by Tana Umaga and Keven Mealamu. O'Driscoll was very seriously injured and could have been crippled for life. Was there any apology forthcoming, or even an admittance that they might have done something wrong or dangerous? Not a bit. Apparently, when Umaga spoke at a Lions reception in the New Zealand parliament he never mentioned O'Driscoll, not even to wish him a speedy recovery. Several Lions walked out in disgust.

Alastair Campbell, that old bruiser more used to dealing with the rough and tumble of politics rather than the serious, and potentially painful, rough and tumble of rugby, was not slow with the *Schadenfreude*. He wrote in the *Sunday Times*:

It is not a noble feeling. But there remains in all of us capacity for the occasional roll around the carpet giggling at the misfortunes of others. For me, that moment came on seeing coach Graham Henry's face crease with angst as the final whistle blew and France went into raptures. So confident had Henry's All Blacks been of victory, that they had not even checked out flight times home. And some 2,000 Kiwis had shelled out almost £4,000 for 'semis-and-final-only' packages, so confident were they that their team would be in both. It's a lot to pay to see England vs. France.

And Campbell could not resist publishing the best jokes he heard or was sent by e-mail:

• Police found the body of a dead man floating in the Tasman Sea. The victim was wearing an All Blacks rugby shirt, stockings and suspenders, a blonde wig, red lipstick and mascara. Police removed the shirt to save his family any embarrassment.

• What's the difference between the All Blacks and a woman's bra? Both have lots of support, but the All Blacks have no cup.

• *Rugby programme for this weekend*
Saturday: France meet England at St Denis, 8pm
Sunday: South Africa meet Argentina at St Denis, 8pm
Monday: New Zealand meet Australia at Charles de Gaulle airport, 1pm

• At least the All Blacks are doing their bit for the earth's carbon footprint. They have offered to drop the Wallabies off on their way home.

• The All Blacks are to be rebranded. From now on they will be known as the Rainbow warriors – sunk by the French again.

• What's the difference between an All Black and an arsonist? An arsonist wouldn't waste five matches.

• Why do the All Blacks always have two to a hotel room when they're on tour? So one can perform the Heimlich manoeuvre when the other one chokes.

• Some All Black supporters die, and as expected they go to hell. The devil notices that they're quite happy, and asks them why.
    They explain: After the lousy weather in New Zealand, we enjoy the warmth.
    Devil thinks: 'I'll fix them' and turns up the heat. He finds the Kiwis with their shirts off enjoying a chop on the barbie and

having a frostie.

'Whenever the weather gets this good in New Zealand, we can't waste it, so this what we do.'

The Devil decides to wipe the smile off their faces by turning the heat down to freezing. He returns to the Kiwis to find them celebrating.

'What now?' he asks.

One explains: 'Well, when hell freezes over, we're sure to win the Rugby World Cup.

• Graham Henry is handed a mobile phone and is told: 'This is Wayne Barnes's phone.'

Henry says: 'How did you know?'

The reply is: 'It had 15 missed calls.'

[Barnes is the Englishman who refereed the New Zealand-France quarter-final.]

• What would the 7th vs. 8th playoff match be called in the World Cup if there were one?

Bledisloe Cup.

CHAPTER EIGHT

Semi-final – France – Blimey, we could win this thing

We shall not flag or fail. We shall go on to the end.

Winston Churchill

– France, not New Zealand, eh? –

By Tuesday 9 October, England had almost stopped congratulating themselves over beating Australia and were looking forward to the next big game which was, to most people's surprise, against France and not New Zealand. I can't remember an occasion when I was surrounded by so many Englishmen wanting France to win a rugby match. It wasn't that we particularly wanted France to win, it was because we thought we had a better chance of beating them than of beating New Zealand. We knew how mercurial France could be. They were fantastic on one of their good days but they had plenty of not-so-good days.

While we enjoyed the delights of Paris, the England

and France rugby squads prepared for their epic battle. Robert Kitson of *The Guardian* listened to the coaches talking about three key men of the England pack: Andrew Sheridan, Simon Shaw and Phil Vickery. Forwards coach Graham Rowntree won 54 England caps himself and said of Sheridan's performance against Australia that it was the best of his career, adding:

'I think he'd agree himself that he's not played like that for England before. He's played well but not that well. He's been desperately unlucky with injuries [breaking his ankle against South Africa last November and pulling a hamstring in the summer] but his application and work ethic are second to none. Now he's got to do it again. If he does that this week – and next week he'll be a world-class player. To merit that description you've got to have physical durability, and mentally you need the focus.'

Next was Simon Shaw, who had suffered in the shadow of Martin Johnson. Indeed, Sir Clive Woodward had told him that he was 'too similar' to Johnson. As Shaw said: 'Most people would think having two Martin Johnsons in your side was a good thing.'

Shaw had finally really come into his own in this World Cup. The coach, John Wells, said:

'We've never had a natural replacement for Johnno with some of the skills Johnno has but at the weekend you saw Simon's ability to play the ball out of the tackle, his support play and his tackling skills.'

Finally there was Phil Vickery, who had not enjoyed a good World Cup until the match against Australia. Of course, he had not helped himself by that moment of madness against the USA. Rowntree said: 'That [the game against Australia] was one of the best games he's played at any level for a long time.'

– Should we worry about Jonny's kicking? –

As they looked forward to France they also looked back at the Australia game to see what improvements could be made. First, there were Jonny Wilkinson's three missed penalties. Rob Andrew said there were extenuating circumstances. Two of the unsuccessful attempts just before half-time had come from the south-east corner of the Stade Vélodrome, where the notorious Mistral was blowing in to reverse the curve of an in-swinging kick and push the ball beyond the far post. Andrew said:

'It was a difficult ground to kick on. It's one of the few international grounds now where the wind plays a part. In the old days you had to deal with it all the time. At the old Twickenham, it was part of the joy of kicking. Jonny was kicking from the hardest area of the field, and there were difficulties from there in practice on Thursday. The other kick he missed was from halfway and only missed by a fraction. I don't think he'll be fazed.'

Actually Jonny Wilkinson *was* a bit fazed, as he made clear when he said:

'It was not just the swirling Marseille wind that made kicking difficult, but the Gilbert ball being used at the tournament.

'As a kicker here you are not completely accountable. Sometimes it is like you are almost hitting and hoping.

'This is a difficult subject and I don't want to make a big deal out of it. But in kicking you naturally want to control as much as you can; you can't ever control the wind and you can't control the pitch conditions. It seems that, at this tournament, the ball is another one of those.'

Wilkinson's record in this World Cup so far was 15 successes out of 24 attempts. This was a 65 per cent rate, well below his normal success rate. Some, most notably All Blacks fly-half Dan Carter, were suggesting that the Gilbert ball not being blown up to the right pressure was partly to blame. Wilkinson refused to comment on that, saying: 'I know how to kick and there's no time for anything else but just to get out there and react. It's the same for everyone.'

England supporters and the media have a tendency to emphasise the importance and significance of Jonny Wilkinson. However, they may have a point, because the statistics show that since he has been playing for England, in the games where he has been present, 49 victories have been achieved in 60 games; whereas in the games where he has not played, England have won only 24 out of 51 games.

– Vital questions –

Writing in *The Guardian*, that genius of a fly-half for France, Thomas Castaignède, posed some key questions for the coming clash and gave his answers:

Are France capable of dealing with the pressure?

Suddenly, from being outsiders after that defeat against Argentina, they are the big favourites because no one envisaged them beating New Zealand. For England, on the other hand, anything is a bonus now because they started the tournament with low expectations – everyone felt they would exit early. It's probably an easier situation for England to manage.

How will England deal with the France back row?

All three who completed the match in Cardiff are on fire, gaining the metres when necessary, defending like demons. Standing out a little above Imanol Harinordoquy and Julien Bonnaire is Thierry Dusautoir, who wasn't meant to be at the tournament but has turned into one of its biggest finds.

How will Bernard Laporte play Beauty and the Beast?

Frédéric Michalak and Sébastien Chabal's arrival on the pitch was key on Saturday night. Personally I'd like to see them on earlier, which leads me to the question of whether Laporte puts Michalak in against England at fly-half. More likely he will keep Fred on the bench because the injury to Pierre Mignoni means there is no scrum-half cover. As for Chabal, I can see the point of bringing him into the action when the opposition are tired, but the way he is playing he deserves to start.

Who will win the battle of the scrum-halves?

Jean-Baptiste Elissalde is a malicious little magician in a world of monsters. When you see him with his top off you can't believe he's part of the rugby world, but his quicksilver brain makes up for his lack of bulk. Against him is Andy Gomarsall, not quite as fast, a man who has resurrected his career in the last few weeks, who has looked great when the England pack have been going forward – but what if they are on the back foot?

Can England deal with France's capacity to switch styles?

On Saturday France set out with a tactic determined by their trainer, a kicking game which didn't work and seemed to instil doubt in the side, until the players changed it round so that when they began to move the ball, putting some tempo in the game, New Zealand weren't able to follow. France are just as strong at present without the ball in hand: look at the way they pushed the All Blacks back as they attempted to attack on Saturday. It's an area they can rely on against England.

How important will Jason Robinson be?

His return from injury was a big factor for the World Cup holders – he's a key element in the team because he gets them moving. They are dependent on Wilkinson's kicking for momentum but Robinson is one of the few who can give them impetus with the ball in hand.

Who will win the set piece?

Given the way England built their win against Australia, the scrum will be crucial, but this is also a French strong point and I'd see Olivier Milloud creating problems if he is over his injury. As for the line-outs, France need to work on this because they were expected to use this area as a weapon against New Zealand but Ali Williams got among them.

Meanwhile, at French headquarters, coach Bernard Laporte said his team had gone back to zero. Funny place to go after they had achieved so much. No, what he meant, he said, was that they were not going to dwell on their fabulous victory over New Zealand but would concentrate solely on their match against England. Laporte thought, or said he thought, that England would be just as difficult to beat as the All Blacks.

And on his side, Rob Andrew was saying the same thing:

'It's all about re-setting sights immediately. And they will do that. They are an incredibly grounded group. There has never been a group of England players that have been under as much pressure as this squad. But they haven't let anything get to them. There will be a nicer feeling in camp this week, but they have got to guard against that too.'

As the weekend approached, people were called on to make their predictions. We were nervous remembering the two warm-up games, especially the second one. The French forwards were clearly a tougher proposition than the Wallabies' pack, and the French defence in both the warm-up games had been very solid. Someone had counted the tackles that France put in against the All Blacks. It was a staggering 299.

Most commentators were reluctant to make a prediction, confining themselves only to saying that it would be a hard-fought, close match. However, former Springbok Nick Mallett was prepared to make predictions. He said, like everyone else, that France would win, but by less than a six-point margin. On the South Africa vs. Argentina match he thought South Africa would just make it.

Will Carling had plenty of experience of playing against France. Indeed, he had taken part in the England victory in Paris in the 1991 World Cup. His view was that:

If they play as well as they did against Australia, they will lose [perhaps he meant *only* as well]. England might have won that match, but they also wasted a lot of chances, and they cannot afford to do that against France. They are not going to dominate the French the way they dominated the Australians, so they have got to capitalise on every opportunity.

– If England get to that last quarter –

Another former England captain, Lawrence Dallaglio, handed out his advice and made some perceptive predictions:

We need to start the game very well to let the French team know it will not be easy for them and they will have to fight for 80 minutes for every little bit of ball, every inch of ground. If the French start well, the crowd are in the game – and if you are getting waves of French attacks it can be very, very difficult.

But if England can get into the game early, like we did against Australia, the team will believe in themselves much more. If England are still there hanging on or, I hope, having the advantage around the hour point it becomes a great place for us to be.

England are happy to be in a close game with 20 minutes to go. If you are the favoured team and it's close, you feel the pressure more. The French will be nervous. It is natural, because they are the home team and it's a semi-final. There is that expectation – so if England can get to the last quarter it is going to be extremely tough for France.

As the great day approached, those of us enjoying the time of our lives in this wonderful country were joined by 30,000 more English invaders. Lots came without tickets but were able to watch in the bars and on big screens. A favourite spot was the Champ de Mars near the Eiffel Tower.

– Never mind the teams, what about the coaches? –

At this stage of the World Cup, the journalists' bosses – and presumably the public – were demanding stories every day, even though the games were now down to a few a week, and only at the weekend. By Wednesday, you can't look back at last weekend's games any more, so you have to start looking forward. You can analyse, and try to interview, each player; you can guess intelligently at the likely strategy and tactics of the teams. What else can you fill those empty columns with? Ah yes, what about the coaches? So that's what Rob Wildman did in the *Daily Telegraph* under the heading ASHTON AND LAPORTE: HOW THEY COMPARE.

Brian Ashton was 61 as opposed to Bernard Laporte's mere 43. Ashton's nickname was 'Coco', apparently because he looked like a clown. Laporte's was 'Bernie le Dingue' (Mad Bernie). Ashton had been a school-teacher, and at Stonyhurst College had coached, among others, former England players Kyran Bracken and Iain Balshaw. Laporte did not say much about his background, but he came from a poor Toulouse family in which there were five sons.

Both had been good club players and, by coincidence, scrum-halves. And both were pragmatic. They, like every-one else, enjoyed open, attacking rugby but knew that winning needed a more cautious approach.

Laporte had the longer and better Test record. Of 96 matches played under him, 62 had been won, 32 lost and two drawn. Under Ashton, England had played 15 matches, won eight and lost seven.

THE TWO TEAMS LINED UP

England   **France**

	Age	Caps	Age	
Jason Robinson	33	49	57	28	Damien Traille
Paul Sackey	27	8	26	26	Vincent Clerc
Mathew Tait	21	17	17	24	David Marty
Mike Catt	36	73	49	29	Yannick Jauzion
Josh Lewsey	30	54	36	29	Cédric Heymans
Jonny Wilkinson	28	63	10	21	Lionel Beauxis
Andy Gomarsall	33	31	28	29	Jean-Baptiste Elis- salde
Andrew Sheridan	27	18	49	31	Olivier Milloud
Mark Regan	35	41	96	34	Raphael Ibañez
Phil Vickery	31	58	68	35	Pieter de Villiers
Simon Shaw	34	41	117	33	Fabien Pelous
Ben Kay	31	51	40	29	Jerome Thion
Martin Corry	34	62	62	33	Serge Betsen
Lewis Moody	29	50	8	25	Thierry Dusautoir
Nick Easter	29	10	36	29	Julien Bonnaire

Subs

	Age	Caps	Age	
George Chuter	31	17	21	24	Dimitri Szarzewski
Matt Stevens	25	19	18	28	Jean-Baptiste Poux
Lawrence Dallaglio	35	83	35	29	Sébastien Chabal
Joe Worsley	30	63	44	27	Imanol Harinord- oquy
Peter Richards	29	10	48	24	Frédéric Michalak
Toby Flood	22	10	65	35	Christophe Dominici
Dan Hipkiss	25	4	31	25	Clément Poitrenaud

The great day arrived and forward Matt Stevens wrote a very interesting piece in the *Daily Telegraph* which gave the rest of us an insight into what the players do in the final 48 hours before the kick-off. I can't imagine what it must be like waiting for a start at 9 o'clock in the evening. I get nervous enough, and I'm not playing.

Apparently, after a very strict diet all week which certainly does not include chocolates and sweets, these are allowed on the day before the match. This is what Stevens wrote:

But I think there's a lot of pressure on both teams this week after the great performances last week. We have adopted the same siege mentality and tried to cut ourselves off from the hype in the outside world. As part of the 22 the preparation is the same but mentally you have to get ready to sit on the bench knowing you could have to come on at any moment and make an impact. It could be a very small difference that you make but it could be crucial.

To help psychologically on the bench we often do something called 'Talking the game' – giving our own commentary on what we would be doing if we were on the field, sometimes quietly, sometimes out loud. It helps to keep focus.

We will try to sleep late and take catnaps during the day to keep our body clocks ready for the kick-off. We will eat breakfast, lunch, a mid-afternoon snack and a pre-match meal. We spend the day trying to think about specific details and not the whole picture. The eventuality of winning or losing is not in our minds and I personally write down a list of what I must do if I come on.

By this time, the two teams had considerable knowledge of each other. They had already played each other three times in the last six months. Furthermore, just as Formula One teams study each other's cars in great detail, so the players will have watched video recordings of their opponents to study their strengths, weaknesses and idiosyncrasies. And, of course, a number of the French team played for English Premiership clubs – for example, Raphael Ibañez who played for Wasps.

– Finally, the game! –

The atmosphere in the Stade de France in Paris is electric as the minutes tick down.

Off we go – and no, I don't believe it, in the second minute a kick by Andy Gomarsall for Josh Lewsey is misread by French centre-turned-full-back Damien Traille, and over goes Lewsey for a try in the corner. It's too good a start, surely. But, we ask ourselves, would you rather be 5–0 up or 5–0 down?

And we nearly scored again when Mark Regan charged down a clearance kick by David Marty and England gained a five-metre scrum. Would we get a push-over try? The French pack gradually began to go backwards and then Nick Easter lost control at the back of the English scrum and the French escaped.

Within five minutes, the French had responded with a penalty given away by Nick Easter coming in at the side; and worse, after another ten minutes, Lionel Beauxis kicked another after Andrew Sheridan, of all people, collapsed a scrum. France were in the lead 6–5. Kicking seemed to be the tactic and Beauxis kept trying dropped goals, effectively kicking away good French possession. It would never have happened in the old days of French adventure and sophistication.

After 25 minutes the talismanic Sébastien Chabal came

on to replace the injured Fabien Pelous. Three minutes later, our Jonny Wilkinson tried to convert a penalty from inside the England half and just fell short. Still they kept trying those drop-goals. Then a mini-disaster: just before half-time, try-scorer Josh Lewsey limped off to be replaced by Dan Hipkiss, or rather for Mathew Tait to move out to the wing and Hipkiss to replace him in the centre.

Early in the second half the French kicked another penalty to make it 9–5. England needed to make sure they got the next score. And they did. Five minutes later, a penalty kick from Wilkinson made it 9–8.

In the 50th minute France made a double substitution. Off went Raphael Ibañez and Lionel Beauxis and on came Dimitri Szarzewski and the fantastic, if mercurial, Frédéric Michalak (it was his magnificent pass that had set up France's winning try against the All Blacks a week earlier). At the same time England brought on Joe Worsley for Lewis Moody and Matt Stevens for the visibly tiring Phil Vickery.

Half-way through the second half and Jonny hit the post with a drop-goal which would have gone over nine times out of ten. Jason Robinson jinked around with the rebound but somehow France cleared it. With fifteen minutes left, on came Lawrence Dallaglio and almost immediately Gomarsall was nearly carried off after a collision with the touch judge.

Now it was substitute Toby Flood's chance to try a drop-goal, and he made a complete hash of it, with the ball barely reaching the try-line. Then England got another penalty after a high tackle by Szarzewski on Jason Robinson, and, with less than ten minutes to go, England were leading 11–9.

They were lucky to be ahead, and could thank replacement Joe Worsley for the most significant tap tackle on Vincent Clerc as he flew towards England's line. This followed a cross-kick from Yannick Jauzion which Julien Bonnaire punched back into Clerc's hands.

But better was to come. Jonny hit one of his trade-mark drop-goals and England were leading 14–9.

It had not been a classic game of rugby. Indeed, the English backs showed virtually no inclination to run with and pass the ball. Kicking it for territory or back to the forwards was the name of the game, and whether we liked it or not, it was effective. Martin Johnson had been dead right. As long as we were in touch, i.e. within one score, with 10 or 15 minutes to go we would probably win. And we did!

Who were the heroes? Everyone said the main man was Jonny Wilkinson and no one could gainsay that he was the man who put the points on the board but, of course, rugby is a 15-man team game and he couldn't do it on his own. Nevertheless, as those who play with and against him say, Wilkinson is more than just a good kicker. Serge Betsen said of him: 'He is still the best number 10 in the world. He has shown everybody that he is still the best, simply the best.'

It is not just his kicking but his passing and tackling which are both of the highest class as well. In fact, a lot of us wish he would do a bit less tackling, knowing how prone to injury he is. Sir Clive Woodward used to fret about it, and with good reason. Nevertheless, it certainly earns him the respect of the rest of his team. They know that he's not just a fancy kicker who takes all the glory.

Naturally, the headlines screamed 'Jonny':

The Independent on Sunday: WILKINSON'S NERVES OF STEEL

The Mail on Sunday: JONNY'S KICK OF GLORY

The Sunday Telegraph: WILKINSON KICKS ENGLAND INTO FINAL

The Observer. GOLDEN BOOT, with a picture of Wilkinson kicking his final penalty, and then ENGLAND IN FINAL OFF JONNY'S BEAUTIFUL BOOT

At least the *Sunday Times* noticed the others and carried a new phrase for England's forwards, shouting: MAGICAL NIGHT FOR GRUMPY OLD MEN.

Outside the scrum was another hero, Jason Robinson. In his 50th match for England he led the team out into the stadium to a huge roar from us all. And he played like a man possessed, catching every high kick with which the French bombarded him. He also came close to scoring a try, and it was he who was attacking when Szarzewski felt obliged to tackle him round the neck, this giving Wilkinson his vital penalty chance with only a few minutes to go.

Up front there were the usual heroes. Andrew Sheridan gave Pieter de Villiers a hard time and Simon Shaw rose above himself again. Finally there was that amazing, match-saving, tap tackle by Joe Worsley. The tackle was obviously critical. French coach Bernard Laporte conceded as much:

'If I kept one image, it would be the dropped goal from Wilkinson, which meant it was finished. The other image was the bootlace tackle on Vincent Clerc. If we scored, we were in the final.'

This is how Worsley himself remembered it:

'I saw about four or five of them lined up on the other side of the pitch so I just took a risk, cut behind the backline and got on my bike. I saw the kick coming and got there as quickly as I could. It was lucky I did because Julien Bonnaire did an amazing tap back to Clerc. I took a line, was slightly stumbling but just managed to dive and get a bit of his ankle. Because he is very quick off the mark I knew he would get away from me unless I went for it there and then. Games are won and lost on millimetres and centimetres and that was an example of that. Moments like that do change games but I am not the only one who did things.'

Of course we were all watching the ball, so we didn't notice Worsley until he dived to make the tackle. I guess that's the benefit of video recordings – you can see what's happening off the ball, which can be highly relevant. It also shows the benefit of fresh legs. Worsley had come on to replace Moody only 15 minutes earlier. Worsley must have felt a lot better than a week earlier, when he conceded the penalty with which Mortlock could have won the game for Australia in the dying moments – if he had converted it.

Others made the point about replacements, but Brian Ashton said he disliked pre-planned tactical replacement. There was always the danger of replacements upsetting the team's rhythm. Not in this case. As Ashton said:

'We have players who know how to win a game. We have the armoury within the squad to get ourselves into positions where we know we can win. That was our big advantage over the French team. The players we brought on could help guide the team through the difficult last 15 minutes of the game compared to the French replacements, who couldn't do that.

'Yet how small the differences between triumph and despair. No more than 12 minutes remained when Joe Worsley, the replacement for Lew Moody whose damaged shoulder forced him off, brought off that ankle-tap that prevented Vincent Clerc scoring. France led 9–8 at that stage and there was little between the electric Toulouse wing and the line, but Clerc stumbled and slowed, enough for the defence to recover and concede only a five-metre scrum.

'The next minute determined the course of the game. England's scrum forced the French to give ground, only a little but it was enough to induce uncertainty. Andy Gomarsall was round to harass and France conceded a penalty.'

There was that garrulous Welshman, Eddie Butler, again, writing in *The Observer*:

From the brilliance of a quarter-final against Australia in Marseille to something unbelievable in Paris. Incredible madness. England beat France. This put the ugly back into rugby. This put England into the final. This was magnificent.

In all the stories of comebacks in sport, few have restarted from such a low point as England. It is hard to describe how ineffably dreadful they were at the start of this World Cup. How they only got worse against the United States. How they fell so hard against the bottom of a deep, deep pit against South Africa.

It is absolutely impossible to state how slim their chances were of defending their title. They were shite.

No one could fathom why England had recovered from the depths of just four weeks earlier. Butler did his best:

You can go out for bonding sessions, hike with Marines or go on the piss for the weekend. Or you can just sit down and say that the rot stops now. And look each other in the eye and say that things change from now on. And mean it. And be mean. And mean it.

And how mean they were. The mighty England pack. Not set-piece triumphant as they had been against Australia, but dogged, scrambling, pesky, obdurate. Horrible. Ugly.

Ugly is so cool. From a state of near collapse, from a starting point of internal turmoil, from a position of conflict between the feeder-system and the national team, England have rebuilt themselves into a global force. It is the rugby comeback of all times.

The template can never be copied. There is no method to this glorious madness. No logic. No class, no style.

Just a group of horrible Englishmen on the wrong side of the Channel refusing to buckle. Refusing to go down the pan when all signposts pointed to the sewer.

Match Data

Scorers: England: Try: Lewsey (2 min). Penalty goals: Wilkinson 2 (47, 75). Dropped goal: Wilkinson (78). France: Penalty goals: Beauxis 3 (8, 18, 44).

Scoring sequence (England first): 5–0, 5–3, 5–6 (half-time), 5–9, 8–9, 11–9, 14–9.

England: J. Robinson (unattached), P. Sackey (Wasps), M. Tait (Newcastle Falcons), M. Catt (London Irish; rep: T. Flood, Newcastle Falcons, 65), J. Lewsey (Wasps; rep: D. Hipkiss, Leicester, 40), J. Wilkinson (Newcastle Falcons), A. Gomarsall (Harlequins; rep: P. Richards, London Irish, 71), A. Sheridan (Sale Sharks), M. Regan (Bristol; rep: G. Chuter, Leicester, 66), P. Vickery (Wasps; rep: M. Stevens, Bath, 56), S. Shaw (Wasps), B. Kay (Leicester), M. Corry (Leicester), L. Moody (Leicester; rep: J. Worsley, Wasps, 54), N. Easter (Harlequins; rep: L. Dallaglio, Wasps, 70).

France: D. Traille (Biarritz), V. Clerc (Toulouse), D. Marty (Perpignan), Y. Jauzion (Toulouse), C. Heymans (Toulouse; rep: C. Dominici, Stade Français, 60); L. Beauxis (Stade Français; rep: F. Michalak, Natal Sharks, 51), J.-B. Elissalde (Toulouse), O. Milloud (Bourgoin), R.

Ibañez (Wasps; rep: D. Szarzewski, Stade Français, 51), P. de Villiers (Stade Français; rep: J.-B. Poux, Toulouse, 66), F. Pelous (Toulouse; rep: S. Chabal, Sale Sharks, 25), J. Thion (Biarritz), S. Betsen (Biarritz; rep: I. Harinordoquy, Biarritz, 67), T. Dusautoir (Toulouse), J. Bonnaire (Clermont-Auvergne).

England		France
1	Tries	0
0	Conversions	0
2	Penalty goals	3
1	Dropped goals	0
83	Tackles	92
9	Missed tackles	9
74	Carries	65
313	Metres	259
8	Defenders beaten	5
1	Clean breaks	1
4	Offload	6
43	Kicks from hand	48
12	Turnovers conceded	11
9	Penalties conceded	5
0	Yellow cards	0
0	Red cards	0
7 from 7	Scrums won	7 from 7
13 from 14	Line-outs won	21 from 22
72 from 74	Rucks won	62 from 67
50 per cent	Possession	50 per cent
47 per cent	Territory	53 per cent

– 'Bravo to the English' –

France took the World Cup to their hearts. There must have been worries when the national team lost the first match to Argentina but, if so, they disappeared when it became clear that France would still qualify for the knock-out stages. And when the team beat the favourites New Zealand in Cardiff, well …

In the semi-final in the Stade de France, whenever we sang about our sweet chariot, the French sang their 'Marseillaise' louder. By the end, I think we were winning both on and off the field.

As fans we had got into the habit of staying in the stadium for some time at the end of each game, soaking up the atmosphere and revelling in our hard-won victories. Nearly all of us wore the white of England (with varying splotches of red), so you could tell this time when *les bleus* had left, and also the yellow and green Australians and the black New Zealanders (some had stayed and resisted the temptation to sell their tickets on the black market). Once they had all gone, we could see how many England supporters there were. I am no good at estimating numbers but it must have been nearly half the stadium, so the 35–40,000 the papers were talking about was perhaps on the button. Certainly it was enough to make a bloody good noise when we sang. Hope the England team could hear in their dressing room.

I had gone to the match with two of my best French friends, brothers as it happened. I sat with one of them and, as we all cheered, Christian was very dignified but a tear did roll down his cheek. He had a flask of Armagnac and said that we must have a drink after every try. When Lewsey scored in only the second minute, it looked as though we might be in for an endurance test, but that of course was the only try, so by the end of the game we felt in need of a drink. Back we went to the Champ de Mars, where we met his brother. They insisted on champagne and, furthermore, insisted on paying. That's what I like about my French friends. They like to win but, if they lose, rugby's only a game, there are other things in life. On we went to the Relais de Cambon: more champagne, and them still insisting on paying.

In stark contrast to the New Zealanders, the French were gracious in defeat. Bernard Lapasset, President of the French Rugby Federation, congratulated the England team, saying:

'Deep down, we wanted to win so bad. This semi-final was only decided by ten minutes of brilliance by an exceptional player [presumably he meant Jonny Wilkinson], who showed what he could do. Bravo to the English, they deserved their win.'

Thierry Dusautoir and Serge Betsen were equally gracious. Dusautoir said: 'It's a huge disappointment. It's the team with the most experience and cool-headedness which won.' And Betsen added: 'They controlled the match when it mattered most.'

And captain Raphael Ibañez said: 'You have to recognise Wilkinson's cool. He showed in those important moments that he is a great player.'

L'Equipe summed up the frustration of all France with UNE FRUSTRATION INFINIE, and then, under the heading LA PUISSANCE ET LA PATIENCE: 'Le match s'est joué sur le fil du rasoir. Et le muscle du pack anglais a fini par user les Bleus.' This time it was TELLEMENT ANGLAIS.

Quotes after a semi-final that left us all exhausted but elated: *L'Equipe*: WATERLOO (below a picture of dejected

French players). Huw Richards in the *Financial Times*, commenting on England's performance in the semi-final and looking forward to the final, wrote: 'South Africa will have seen nothing to frighten them, but nor did the Australians or the French in England's earlier perform-ances.'

The Gilbert rugby ball controversy would not go away and, to assuage people's fears that the balls were not being blown up to the pressure recommended by the manufacturer, not only were checks made, but Wilkinson was allowed to practice with the six balls to be used in the match against France. After a lengthy session he declared himself 'happy'. Just what they wanted to hear, as they remembered that Wilkinson had scored all 24 points with his boot when England beat France 24–7 in the semi-final in the 2003 World Cup.

And then, lo and behold, one of the balls which Wilkinson used for a penalty in the game against France was *not* a match ball. Fortunately, he noticed and rejected it. Rob Andrew said later:

'Jonny was pretty vigilant. Training balls can lose pressure and shape over weeks of constant use. The match balls are marked and numbered from one to six: the ones used on Saturday also had 'semi-final' and the date written on them. Having been alert to the situation, he was right to insist on having a match ball to kick.'

After this amazing game which, as we all agreed, was not pretty – though by God, it was gripping – some of the England players struggled to come to terms with what they had achieved. Lewis Moody managed 'surreal', Simon Shaw admitted that he 'didn't know what was going on', and Phil Vickery said: 'Sport doesn't always make sense.' On the beaten French side, the Toulouse winger Cédric Heymans said: 'Our dream has flown away; reality has set in. It makes you wonder whether beating the All Blacks was worth it when your reward is to be hurt as badly as this.'

And certainly, within a few days, Bernard Laporte would be wondering whether it was all worth it, because the French press, having praised him to the skies after the defeat of the All Blacks, now tore him apart.

Laporte himself felt that the key moment in the match was the early departure of his long-established lock forward Fabien Pelous with a rib injury. (If he was right, it was not only Wilkinson's kicking that won the game but his tackling as well, because it was Jonny's juddering tackle that felled Pelous in the 26th minute.) Laporte was forced to bring on Sébastien Chabal probably half an hour before he intended or wanted to. Laporte said later:

'Chabal did well but we wanted to use him with 25 minutes to go. He had to play a different game because he came on so early and he lost a lot of his importance to us. Pelous going off was a defining moment … We did not set out to play a kicking game and said at half-time that we needed to move the ball and inject some rhythm into our game but we failed to do so.'

Given time to reflect, some of the English players came up with more rational thoughts about their revival from those dreadful days a month ago. Joe Worsley offered his reasoning:

'We knew that our preparation in the four years since the World Cup had not been great. Everything was topsy-turvy with changes in the management and the team, and we started this tournament poorly. We had a long meeting as a group after the South Africa game and resolved to go about things differently. The management decided to change the way we trained because we were getting turned over on our own possession far too often and were unable to get the ball wide quickly, and we all agreed that we needed to adopt a different style of play. We have improved in every game since. We did not make any rash promises but took all the criticism on the chin and moved forward together.'

Mike Catt agreed, and also mentioned that critical meeting after the South Africa game:

'Exactly what was said in the heart-to-heart that morning will come out in the wash one day. We have been a different team since then, from a management and a playing perspective, but it is still completely different from four years ago. We were the favourites in Australia and expected to win every game. This year no one fancied us and I have to admit that, considering where we were last month, I am surprised that we are in the final.

'If you had asked me then whether I thought we had a chance, I would have said never. What's happened? Fate, I suppose. I just hope there is one more surprise to come. Beating Australia boosted our confidence hugely and there is still more to come.'

CHAPTER NINE

Final – South Africa – Bloody good try

You ask, what is our aim? Victory, victory at all costs.

Winston Churchill

– Would the 'grumpy old men' make it? –

As the final approached and we all still wondered how these guys, who played such a shambles a month ago, had beaten two of the best teams in the world supposedly on cracking form, Paul Rees in *The Guardian* put together a very useful history, player by player, of where they had been two years ago:

Supposedly finished were:

Jason Robinson, who had just announced his retirement from international rugby

Mike Catt, who had lost his place in the England side (I was at Twickenham when he suffered the humiliation, and we the embarrassment, of him being booed)

Mark Regan, who had also announced his retirement from international rugby

Lawrence Dallaglio, yet another who had retired from international rugby.

Constantly dogged by injuries were:

Jonny Wilkinson, what an agonising time he was enduring

Andy Gomarsall, plagued by injuries which drained his confidence

Andrew Sheridan, brilliant when fit but also afflicted with injuries

Phil Vickery, serious back injuries

Matt Stevens, also plagued with injuries

Joe Worsley, who was in and out of the England team and suffered a recurring knee injury.

Struggling with the authorities were:

Lewis Moody, who had been sent off against Samoa and given a lengthy ban

George Chuter, ruled out of autumn 2005 Tests after a second citing.

Considered to be past their best were:

Simon Shaw
Ben Kay

Up and coming but no impact as yet were:

Paul Sackey
Matthew Tait, who had made an unconvincing debut against Wales
Josh Lewsey, who had been in and out of the team
Nick Easter
Peter Richards
Toby Flood
Dan Hipkiss

The only player who was going well then and continued to do so was **Martin Corry**.

The brilliant Simon Barnes summed up all our sentiments and feelings when he wrote in *The Times*, happily easy to buy everywhere in France now, on the day before the final:

The New Zealanders can't understand how they are out. Nor can the Aussies. Nor the French. But England can't understand how they're in. It is, as Vickery so candidly remarked, beyond sense. Sport does that. Not often, not regularly, but every now and then sport takes leave of its senses and gives us a result that simply can't be explained, which leaves psychologists, conspiracy theorists, coaches, columnists and players scratching their heads and wondering what the bloody hell is going on.

And people were still criticising England and saying it would not be good for the sport. Luckily for them, none of these critics were anywhere near me or any of the rest of the faithful fans around me. Not playing enough rugby? Obviously Brian Ashton felt they were in danger of playing too much rugby. Apparently he sent a message to the team in the second half of the semi-final to cut out the 'rugby' and kick more.

A lot of the flak was coming from the southern hemisphere, though Jake White, the Springboks' coach, thought it was all a load of rubbish:

'A couple of weeks ago the four southern hemisphere sides were going to dominate. All this talk of north versus south is irrelevant when it comes down to the final. It's about England and South Africa now and they [England] must be in a great mindset. They were dead and buried, they came back and beat Australia and France on consecutive weekends.'

– 'A grade one strain' –

The first big worry to beset England in their preparations for the final against South Africa – who had run out comfortable winners over Argentina as nerves appeared to get to the Pumas, causing them to make some elementary mistakes – was the hamstring injury to try-scorer Josh Lewsey. Would he recover in time?

The answer came on the Monday, and it was unfortunately – no, he won't recover in time. The medical team described his injury as a 'grade one strain'. It was a very great shame for Lewsey himself, who said:

'I'm devastated, as you'd expect. It's cruel but that's what sport does to you, even though you sacrifice a lot to put it first in your life. You set yourself goals and sometimes those goals aren't achieved through no fault of your own. To create an opportunity and then have that opportunity taken from you … it's hard to take. But the beauty of a team game like rugby is that everyone has a role, whether or not they're among those lucky enough to take the field … The only thing that matters to me now is that we win the final.'

And it was a shame for England because Lewsey had played in all the matches since they started winning against Samoa.

A more positive note, for French hoteliers anyway, was that they could double or even treble their prices. And talking of prices, in spite of Lewis Hamilton's excellent chances of becoming Formula One Drivers' Champion, the odds on Jonny Wilkinson becoming BBC Sports Personality of the Year dropped from 20–1 to 3–1.

By Monday, Brian Ashton was being asked all sorts of questions about how he would approach the big game. He was reminded that there was plenty of flak coming from many quarters, but most notably from capitals in the southern hemisphere, that England were not playing proper rugby but were just concentrating on tight defence, strong scrummaging and, above all, kicking for field possession. He was as close to contemptuous of these remarks as he ever gets:

'We're approaching these games in the way we think we can best win them. I don't believe a team needs this thing called a game plan. What I believe in is adaptability. I back the players I send on to the pitch and I give them a fair amount of responsibility. Yes, we have a framework in respect of how we want to play, and there might be one or two directives from the coaching team as to how we feel a particular match might be won. But I hate coaching by dictatorship and I'm not a control freak in any sense of the phrase. I bet some of those people talking about our "style" of rugby from thousands of miles away wish they were sitting where I'm sitting now.'

In the run-up to the big game every one wanted to have their say or, more often than not, were pressed into saying something because the public wanted to read about it – and therefore the journalists had to write about it.

The South African Rugby Union (SARFU) appeared to drop a goal against themselves when they advertised the position of national coach and said applications had to be lodged by Friday, the day before the final. Did this mean Jake White would have to break off organising his team for the biggest game of their lives to work on his application for his own job? Apparently not, because his contract allowed for negotiations after the tournament before the end of his term on 31 December 2007. Nevertheless, the timing seemed bizarre, and White was clearly annoyed about it:

'When you win the World Cup, you've got to go, there's no more you can achieve – and if you don't, they probably want you to go anyway. If my contract doesn't get renewed and England come to me with a proposal to coach them one day, I would be crazy not to accept it.'

Whatever, England will not have been unhappy to notice that all was not sweetness and light in the South African camp. For those South Africans concentrating on the game on Saturday and nothing beyond, centre François Steyn noted the danger of Jonny Wilkinson, saying:

'We have not yet decided on a special plan [for Wilkinson]. He is a key factor, but England have great forwards too. Jonny's drop-goals are perfect. He brings a calmness to their team.'

– The experts give their views –

South Africa's technical adviser and Australia's coach in the 2003 World Cup, Eddie Jones, felt that Wilkinson was not as dominant a player as he had been in 2003 but that he was still a formidable presence who kicked 'reasonably well' and could 'drop a field goal here and there'. He was more keen to talk about his own team:

'South Africa will play how we need to play. We are able to play a tight grinding game if we need to and kick for field position. If we need to shift the ball, then we will shift the ball. That's how rugby should be played.

'It's all about getting your preparation focused this week and not letting distractions get to you. The preparation for a final is the easy bit because you have been together for six to seven weeks and it's about reinforcing the good things and not allowing negative thoughts or different views to creep in.

'The game has become a lot narrower in this World Cup and therefore the No. 9 and No. 10 are much more influential. It is not simply a question of the Springboks playing it tight in the final because of the risk of losing the ball in the breakdown. You might as well close the field down and make the pitch 15 metres wide. I think the good thing about South Africa is that we have scored tries and have been able to use the ball given the opportunity. That's going to be a significant factor in the final. If you cancel out the set piece and cancel out the defence, then your ability to score tries is going to be massive.'

All the experts were asked their opinion. Brian Viner interviewed former England captain Will Carling. Carling was a very successful England captain, leading the team to three Grand Slams and also to the final of the 1991 World Cup. His comments were worth listening to. Although he did not expect England to beat South Africa, he admitted that he had not expected them to beat Australia or France either, and said:

'Sometimes, sides get such momentum in a competition that they become unstoppable. I think England have almost reached that point, and I have no doubt that they have the personnel to beat South Africa. If they can just stay in contention, and it comes to the last 10 or 15 minutes, then who would you want in the No. 10 shirt: Butch James or Jonny Wilkinson?'

He continued:

'The back-row contest is crucial. South Africa get a lot of confidence from those big, powerful ball carriers, but if the England back row can stop them on the gain line, then South Africa will have to go to the midfield to create momentum, where I think they'll miss [the centre, Jean] de Villiers massively. [François] Steyn is hugely talented, but he's mercurial. He can have shockers, and the same with Butch James ...'

What did Carling think of South Africa's glamorous full-back, Percy Montgomery?

'He's been in incredible form, kicking-wise. But Argentina kicked very poorly to him. They gave him a lot of time under the high ball. We mustn't do that and we mustn't kick too long. We need to arrive, man on ball, as quickly as possible. And try the odd little grubber to cut Habana out of the game.'

Are you reading this, England squad?

Carling didn't make any comment about the line-outs, but that was clearly going to be a critical area. Ben Kay didn't have any doubts about that, and he realised that he and Shaw would have one hell of a battle on their hands trying to cope with Victor Matfield, who is 6ft 7in tall and weighs 17st 14lbs and has 66 international caps, and Bekkies Botha, also 6ft 7in and 18st 8lb with 43 caps. Of these two, Kay said:

'They are very athletic jumpers, they know who's going in the air, they get in the air and cause you problems. It's an area they look to dominate. We'll look to compete a bit harder in the air than against France.'

And, if we wanted to hear what Will Carling had to say and hope that the England squad might listen to his advice, then we certainly wanted to hear what Sir Clive Woodward had to bring to the party. On the Thursday before the final, *The Times* duly obliged. In fact, Woodward did not proffer much advice, and I guess he thought that, as the former coach, it would not be right to do so. However, he doubted that South Africa would try dropped goals from huge distances as Australia and France had done. Having said that, he went on:

'My thoughts are with them every step of the way and I just hope we see a second winner's medal around Vickery's neck. A wet, rainy night would be another welcome gift from our friends in France.'

And he put his neck on the line by concluding: 'England to win by three points.'

What did another former England captain, now a replacement on the bench in the final, Lawrence Dallaglio, have to say?

'France came intent on kicking the ball in the air and we didn't think Australia used their most dangerous players. We have worked out a way of beating the opposition in front of us. With South Africa that will be much harder to do because they are a balanced side with strength right across the field.'

Whatever our hopes were, the stark facts of the recent matches against South Africa did not make for pretty reading for an Englishman:

- Four defeats in the last four games

- A score-line deficit of 149–32 in the last three games

- A 36–0 hammering in the pool game.

Moreover, in the tournament as a whole, South Africa had scored 33 tries and we had scored 12.

On the Wednesday, having absorbed the bad news that Josh Lewsey would not be available, and established that everyone else was fit, Ashton announced his team and replacements for Saturday. There were no surprises. I think we had all guessed that he would make a straight swap of Mark Cueto for Lewsey rather than put Dan Hipkiss in the centre and move Matthew Tait out to the wing, and this he duly did.

Brian Ashton said the decision had been a 'pretty close call', and 'it was that he [Cueto] has played a lot of international rugby in the back three. We expect a fair old bombardment and the experience of someone who has played international rugby in that position is important.'

Cueto himself said:

'I feel I've got a lot to prove. The World Cup hasn't gone how I would have liked personally. I feel I have a point to prove to myself, my family and friends. To get an opportunity to do that in the final is a special chance.'

The team read:

	Position	Age	Caps	Club
Backs				
Jason Robinson	15	33	50	Unattached
Paul Sackey	14	27	9	Wasps
Matthew Tait	13	21	18	Newcastle Falcons
Mike Catt	12	36	74	London Irish
Mark Cueto	11	27	23	Sale Sharks
Jonny Wilkinson	10	28	64	Newcastle Falcons
Andy Gomarsall	9	33	32	Harlequins
Forwards				
Andrew Sheridan	1	28	19	Sale Sharks
Mark Regan	2	35	42	Bristol
Phil Vickery	3	31	59	Wasps
Simon Shaw	4	34	42	Wasps
Ben Kay	5	31	52	Leicester
Martin Corry	6	34	63	Leicester
Lewis Moody	7	29	51	Leicester
Nick Easter	8	29	11	Harlequins
Replacements				
George Chuter		31	18	Leicester
Matt Stevens		25	20	Bath

	Age	Caps	Club
Replacements *cont.*			
Lawrence Dallaglio	35	84	Wasps
Joe Worsley	30	64	Wasps
Peter Richards	29	11	Wasps
Toby Flood	22	11	Newcastle Falcons
Dan Hipkiss	25	5	Leicester

As the pressure for tickets for the final and for accommodation built up to almost frenzied levels, I felt almost smug that I had had faith and had got myself organised with both a ticket and a hotel bed long before the World Cup kicked off. My friends and I watched in amazement as ticket prices soared to £2,000. Justin Hopwood of English Rugby Travel said they had received 3,000 enquiries in the hour after the end of the semi-final. The hospitality agencies could not meet the demand for £2,000 per person for ticket and hotel packages. Eurostar laid on seven extra trains so that it could carry 30,000 passengers on Saturday. If you wanted to go in style, International Air Charter, based in Kent, would rent a six-seat jet for a return trip for £6,000 or an eight-seater for £8,000.

Against England would be this South African team:

	Position	Age	Caps	Club
Backs				
Percy Montgomery	15	33	93	Natal Sharks
J.P. Pietersen	14	21	14	Natal Sharks

Jacque Fourie	13	24	36	Golden Lions
François Steyn	12	20	15	Natal Sharks
Bryan Habana	11	24	34	Blue Bulls
Butch James	10	28	25	Natal Sharks
Fourie du Preez	9	25	37	Blue Bulls

Forwards

Os du Randt	1	35	79	Free State Cheetahs
John Smit	2	29	73	Natal Sharks
C.J. van der Linde	3	27	46	Free State Cheetahs
Bakkies Botha	4	28	43	Blue Bulls
Victor Matfield	5	30	66	Blue Bulls
Schalk Burger	6	24	37	Western Stormers
Juan Smith	7	26	40	Free State Cheetahs
Danie Rossouw	8	29	30	Blue Bulls

Replacements

Bismarck du Plessis	23	4	Free State Cheetahs
Jamie du Plessis	23	5	Natal Sharks
Johann Muller	27	17	Natal Sharks
Wikus van Heerden	28	8	Blue Bulls
Ruan Pienaar	23	14	Natal Sharks
Andre Pretorius	28	25	Golden Lions
Wynand Olivier	24	17	Blue Bulls

– Here we go! –

After a very long day spent in suspended animation, we finally went to the Stade de France again. What must it have been like for the players? Jason Robinson, for one, had said how much he hated these 9pm kick-offs. For his money, he would like every game to start at 12 noon. Unfortunately, television audiences rule the roost. During the day, it was almost as if the whole of England had invaded Paris. Around the Eiffel Tower there was not a Frenchman in sight – just thousands and thousands of English. At least half of them can't have had a ticket, nor a room for the night for that matter. It was going to be a long weekend.

To help keep us going and to tempt us into backing our hunches with some money, these were the odds being offered by Ladbrokes:

To win the World Cup: South Africa 4–11
                                                  England 2–1

England to win the World Cup
and Lewis Hamilton to win the
F1 Drivers' Championship: 3–1

South Africa to win the World Cup
and Hamilton not to win the
F1 Drivers' Championship: 4–1

Why didn't I have a bet on that to temper my disappointment just a little bit?

First try scorer:	Bryan Habana	8–1
	J.P. Pietersen	10–1
	Paul Sackey	12–1
	Jason Robinson	14–1
	Jaque Fourie	14–1
	Mark Cueto	14–1
	Percy Montgomery	14–1
	Wynand Olivier	14–1
	François Steyn	14–1

– The line-outs would be key –

If there was one area where the South Africans had been infinitely superior to all their opponents it was in the line-out. They had won almost every single one of their own throws and had stolen about 30 per cent of their opposition's throws. England had to improve on that. Certainly they had to win all their own throws and possibly steal one of two of South Africa's.

Unfortunately, the very first England throw-in was lost when Bakkies Botha leaned across Simon Shaw to win the ball. Worse, the second England throw was lost too. The message went out to the South African backs – kick for touch and we have a fair chance of not only gaining a big chunk of ground but winning back possession as well.

Even worse was to come shortly when Mathew Tait, still in his own 22, attempted to cut back, slipped and was smothered by South African forwards. A penalty was the result and Percy Montgomery does not miss from the centre of the field on the opposing 22 line. So, we were 3–0 down and already seriously worried about the line-outs. (By the final whistle, Botha and the superb Victor Matfield had won seven England throws.)

England continued to enjoy territorial advantage but could not turn it into points. However, after 13 minutes they did secure a penalty after Simon Shaw grabbed hold of a high, hanging kick and set up an England attack. Although Bryan Habana brought down Paul Sackey with a thumping tackle, the South Africans infringed and Jonny Wilkinson converted the difficult chance from near the touch-line: 3–3.

Then Lewis Moody decided to make a sly trip and upended Butch James. Alain Rolland, who sounds French but is in fact Irish, had not been asked to referee the final because he has faulty peripheral vision, and he duly spotted the infringement – 6–3 to South Africa.

England responded by driving back into the South African half and set up a dropped-goal chance for Wilkinson. Unfortunately his attempt drifted wide. South Africa also lost a chance to move further ahead when a long-range penalty from François Steyn also went wide. However, shortly afterwards, Steyn made a dazzling run past Mike Catt, Jonny Wilkinson and Phil Vickery to take South Africa into England's 22. England managed to stop South African captain John Smit a yard from their line, but gave away a penalty in the ensuing ruck. Percy Montgomery made it 9–3, and that's how it stayed until half-time.

At the beginning of the second half, with Matt Stevens on in place of Phil Vickery, Mathew Tait made what I think was the best break by an England back in the whole tournament. The movement did not start very well because Gomarsall's pass was actually bouncing on the ground when Tait gathered it – perhaps the South African defence was confused. Whatever, Tait surged through and after a superb run was only just stopped five metres short of the South African try-line by the brilliant lock, Victor Matfield. From the ensuing ruck Andy Gomarsall passed out left to Mark Cueto, who dived over the line to score just as he was tackled by Danie Rossouw, the big number 8. We all jumped up – brilliant!

However, to our horror, Alain Rolland called on the Australian match official, Stuart Dickinson, to adjudicate.

– Was it a try? –

In truth it was impossible for any of us, seeing it at a distance with the naked eye, to tell. Initially, looking at some of the replays on the screen, it looked as though it was a try because, as Cueto touched down, although his foot was over the line, it was in the air. But then another showed his foot on the line milliseconds before he touched it down. By such millimetres and milliseconds are games won and lost.

Of course, there were howls of protest around the Stade de France but, in retrospect, it was a good decision. And he took his time. It was three agonising minutes for all of us there and, no doubt, for the millions watching on television in England and South Africa. Paddy O'Brien, the referees' manager for the International Rugby Board, said later:

'It was an absolutely brilliant decision by the television match official and there is a great photo of his [Cueto's] foot just on the line prior to grounding the ball. There is no issue, there is no doubt. It was a perfect illustration of television match official protocol. Our big thing is that we've got the technology. Let's use it.

People may criticise officials for taking time, but it's better that it's correct. Cueto himself was not convinced, saying:

'You generally have a good feeling straightaway when you think you have scored a try. I thought it was a legitimate try, and I went straight back to the restart. As long as I live I will tell people it was a try.'

Wilkinson was his usual sporting self:

'It looked okay, but I'm sure the guy making the decision made a good one. Maybe in other games it would have gone our way, but this one didn't.'

In all the excitement we had forgotten that the referee was playing the advantage rule while this prolonged try attempt, and even more prolonged investigation, were taking place. He now awarded a penalty, and at least we now gained three points as Wilkinson converted it. Mind you, he nearly missed it. The ball bounced through off a post. So at least 9–3 became 9–6, but it was nowhere near as good as 9–8 or even 10–9 to us. Furthermore, the effect of scoring such a scintillating try would surely have been profound. If England had indeed gone into the lead, the South Africans would have had to alter their game plan.

As it was, yet another Montgomery penalty put the South Africans 12–6 in front, and shortly afterwards the valiant Jason Robinson had to retire with a crocked shoulder. He was replaced by Dan Hipkiss. Brian Ashton now sent on Toby Flood to replace Mike Catt. England were looking potentially threatening when they conceded yet another kickable penalty. It was long range, but this time François Steyn made no mistake. I was outraged by this penalty, awarded apparently for Ben Kay crossing – and I imagine many others were too. It seemed to me that he was getting out of the way of one of his own forwards. Now England were more than a converted try behind. They needed that and either a penalty or a dropped goal.

– It was all about South Africa's defence –

They attacked and attacked with the magnificent Andrew Sheridan to the fore, but to no avail. South Africa won 15–6. They had played it tough, stuck to their game plan. Martin Corry said that the World Cup would be won by the team with the best defence. He was proved right. The speedy Bryan Habana was never part of that plan and he scarcely featured. He remained the tournament's leading try-scorer, but he was never going to score any in this match unless the English gifted him them the way the Argentineans had in the semi-final. As for the South African defence, Mathew Tait very nearly breached it, and what a hero he would have been if he had, but no one else came near. We should remember that when South Africa won their final against the All Blacks in 1995, they kept out Jonah Lomu, even though Lomu had run through every other team. In fact Lomu never scored a try against South Africa. What a pity the slight Mathew Tait did not score. He could have lived on the comparison with Lomu for the rest of his life.

The England players were gracious in defeat. We have already seen that Wilkinson was not going to complain about the disputed Cueto try decision, and he now said:

'The South Africa team deserved to win – they've been fantastic all tournament.'

Captain Phil Vickery said: 'I can't fault anyone – the players, the supporters. We've had a magical time here. Fair play to South Africa. They were the better team and this is their victory.'

Coach Brian Ashton's early reaction was to say: 'They [England] did fantastically well getting in to the final. In days to come, they'll reflect on what they've done and be really proud of themselves.'

When asked if he thought the disallowed Cueto try was a turning point, Ashton replied:

'It would be easy to say with hindsight it was a turning point. It was a big moment certainly but it would be hard to justify why it would have been a turning point. I'm incredibly proud of the players, who put up such a fight. I thought we were pretty unlucky on a couple of occasions [presumably the Kay penalty and the lack of one to England, also for crossing, shortly afterwards] and the scoreline of 15–6 didn't reflect the difference between the two sides, but I have to offer my congratulations to South Africa.'

Given time to think about the try that wasn't, Cueto said he was flabbergasted by the decision and was still adamant that he had scored:

I scored. I'll believe it until my dying day. My gut feeling when I went over was that I'd made it – you develop a sense of these things – and I didn't think for a moment it would be disallowed. I went low for the line because of Danie Rossouw coming across for the tackle and as he went over me I lifted my left leg because I knew I was tight to the line.

You could see from everyone's body language that there

were no doubts. When we went all the way back down the field, it was because we genuinely expected the Boks to be restarting from halfway. Teams don't do that to score psychological points or attempt to influence the decision. They do it because they've scored.

As for Mathew Tait, he could scarcely believe that he had managed to beat all the three-quarters only to be tackled by a second-row forward, Victor Matfield (Matfield did enough damage to us in the line-outs without doing this to us as well). Tait said later:

I wouldn't have minded quite so much if I'd been caught by Bryan Habana. Matfield? A second-row forward? It takes some believing.

The English press were kind to England, and quite right too. They were not the best team in the tournament. Indeed, they were possibly only the fifth or sixth best. In August, if you had been asked to put the top six teams in order you might have written down:

1. New Zealand

2. Australia

3. South Africa

4. France

5. Ireland

6. England

But who got to the final, beating Australia and the France who had already beaten New Zealand?

As David Walsh said in the *Sunday Times*:

There was no shame in defeat. This was an England team that punched above its weight and exceeded expectations. They did themselves proud and to watch them as they flailed at the South Africa defence throughout that second half was to be reminded of the fighter who knows he is going to be beaten but won't accept it.

– They were heroes –

Even the leaders in the Sundays the day after the final waxed lyrical about what heroes they were.

The *Independent on Sunday*, under the headline A TRI-UMPH, AFTER ALL, FOR DOGGEDNESS, wrote:

As a country, we don't do flair; it's too much like dads dancing at discos. And flamboyance is at odds with our temperament, which has been formed by, among other elements, fear of invasion, religious conditioning, the weather, waiting in queues – and which can best be expressed in a single word, 'dogged-ness'.

It was doggedness that won us our only football World Cup back in 1966. The country may have been swinging and dedi-cated to following fashion, but the 11 players who did duty that July day included two balding brothers with comb-overs, the Charltons, a ginger-haired short-arse, Alan Ball, and a toothless but vicious terrier, Nobby Stiles.

Even Lewis Hamilton who now has one hand on the World Drivers' Championship at São Paulo today has, for all his youth-ful brilliance, deployed English pragmatism in earning more points by finishing in the places than he has in winning just four Grands Prix.

The *Sunday Times*, under the headline PRIDE OF ENGLAND, wrote:

And so the extraordinary adventure is over. The most remarkable comeback in English sporting history reached its amazing climax. Just five weeks ago, after South Africa thrashed England 36–0, the rugby pundits wrote that 'England rugby is rotten' and 'the chariot is destined for the scrapyard'. Well, the Stade de France last night was some scrapyard. The grumpy old yeomen of England had ground their way into the stadium with a dogged, curmudgeonly display of bulldog fighting spirit that should make every Briton's chest a little bit more puffed out this morning. And we mean every Briton. For the spirit displayed by the England team, despite the defeat last night, was one that is reflected right across the British Isles. Sporting analogies can be taken too far, but England's use of their limited abilities and their sheer bloodymindedness getting to the final was a characteristic that has shown itself throughout British history.

The Guardian did not miss the opportunity to compare the England rugby team with England's 'lacklustre football team' and continued:

This tournament has been an exhibition in sporting derring-do, thrilling the good-natured fans who flocked to France without incident in a manner football must envy.

– The statistics –

Pool A

	P	W	D	L	F	A	BP	Pts
S. Africa	4	4	0	0	189	47	3	19
England	4	3	0	1	108	88	2	14
Tonga	4	2	0	2	89	96	1	9
Samoa	4	1	0	3	69	143	1	5
USA	4	0	0	4	61	142	1	1

Pool B

	P	W	D	L	F	A	BP	Pts
Australia	4	4	0	0	215	41	4	20
Fiji	4	3	0	1	114	136	3	15
Wales	4	2	0	2	168	105	4	12
Japan	4	0	1	3	64	210	1	3
Canada	4	0	1	3	51	120	0	2

Pool C

	P	W	D	L	F	A	BP	Pts
N. Zealand	4	4	0	0	309	34	4	20
Scotland	4	3	0	1	116	66	2	14
Italy	4	2	0	2	85	117	1	9
Romania	4	1	0	3	40	161	1	5
Portugal	4	0	0	4	38	209	1	1

Pool D

	P	W	D	L	F	A	BP	Pts
Argentina	4	4	0	0	143	33	2	18
France	4	3	0	1	188	37	3	15
Ireland	4	2	0	2	64	82	1	9
Georgia	4	1	0	3	50	111	1	5
Namibia	4	0	0	4	30	212	0	0

Pool		Venue
	Friday 7 September	
D	France 12–17 Argentina	Stade de France
	Saturday 8 September	
C	New Zealand 76–14 Italy	Marseille
B	Australia 91–3 Japan	Lyon
A	England 28–10 United States	Lens
	Sunday 9 September	
B	Wales 42–17 Canada	Nantes
A	South Africa 59–7 Samoa	Parc des Princes
C	Scotland 59–10 Portugal	St Etienne
D	Ireland 32–17 Namibia	Bordeaux
	Tuesday 11 September	
D	Argentina 33–3 Georgia	Lyon
	Wednesday 12 September	
A	United States 15–25 Tonga	Montpellier
B	Japan 31–35 Fiji	Toulouse
C	Italy 24–18 Romania	Marseille
	Friday 14 September	
A	England 0–36 South Africa	Stade de France
	Saturday 15 September	
C	New Zealand 108–13 Portugal	Lyon

Pool		Venue
B	Wales 20–32 Australia	Cardiff
D	Ireland 14–10 Georgia	Bordeaux
	Sunday 16 September	
B	Fiji 29–16 Canada	Cardiff
A	Samoa 15–19 Tonga	Montpellier
D	France 87–10 Namibia	Toulouse
	Monday 17 September	
C	Scotland 42–0 Romania	Murrayfield
	Wednesday 19 September	
C	Italy 31–5 Portugal	Parc des Princes
	Thursday 20 September	
B	Wales 72–18 Japan	Cardiff
	Friday 21 September	
D	France 25–3 Ireland	Stade de France
	Saturday 22 September	
A	South Africa 30–25 Tonga	Lens
A	England 44–22 Samoa	Nantes
D	Argentina 63–3 Namibia	Marseille
	Sunday 23 September	
B	Australia 55–12 Fiji	Montpellier
C	Scotland 0–40 New Zealand	Murrayfield
	Tuesday 25 September	
B	Canada 12–12 Japan	Bordeaux
C	Romania 14–10 Portugal	Toulouse
	Wednesday 26 September	
D	Georgia 30–0 Namibia	Lens
A	Samoa 25–21 United States	St Etienne
	Friday 28 September	
A	England 36–20 Tonga	Parc des Princes

Pool		Venue
	Saturday 29 September	
C	New Zealand 85–8 Romania	Toulouse
B	Australia 37–6 Canada	Bordeaux
B	Wales 34–38 Fiji	Nantes
C	Scotland 18–16 Italy	St Etienne
	Sunday 30 September	
D	France 64–7 Georgia	Marseille
D	Ireland 15–30 Argentina	Parc des Princes
A	South Africa 64–15 United States	Montpellier

Quarter-finals

	Venue
Saturday 6 October	
Australia 10–12 England	Marseille
New Zealand 18–20 France	Cardiff
Sunday 7 October	
South Africa 37–20 Fiji	Marseille
Argentina 19–13 Scotland	Stade de France

Semi-finals

	Venue
Saturday 13 October	
England 14–9 France	Stade de France
Sunday 14 October	
South Africa 37–13 Argentina	Stade de France

Third place play-off

	Venue
Friday 19 October	
France 10–34 Argentina	Parc des Princes

Final

	Venue
Saturday 20 October	
England 6–15 South Africa	Stade de France

– More statistics –

Leading points-scorers   Pts

Percy Montgomery SA	105
Félipe Contepomi Arg	91
Jonny Wilkinson Eng	67
Nick Evans NZ	50
Jean-Baptiste Elissalde Fr	47

Leading try-scorers

Bryan Habana SA	8
Drew Mitchell Aus	7
Shane Williams Wal	6
Doug Howlett NZ	6
Vincent Clerc Fr	5

Most tries

New Zealand	48
South Africa	33
Australia	31
France	27
Argentina	23

Most points in a game

Nick Evans NZ (vs. Portugal)	33
Percy Montgomery SA (vs. Samoa)	29
J.-B. Elissalde Fr (vs. Namibia)	27
Matt Giteau Aus (vs. Fiji)	27
Jonny Wilkinson Eng (vs. Samoa)	24

Yellow cards

United States	4
Argentina	4
South Africa	4
Fiji	3
Italy	3

Line-outs (success on own, opposition)

N. Zealand 63/66 (95.5%), 11/50 (22%)
Australia 59/62 (95.2%), 22/76 (28.9%)
Wales 55/59 (93.2%), 6/45 (13.3%)
S. Africa 83/90 (92.2%), 33/117 (28.2%)
Scotland 75/84 (89.3%), 21/82 (25.6%)

Scrums (success on own, opposition)

Italy 31/32 (96.9%), 6/27 (22.2%)
England 47/49 (95.9%), 9/68 (13.2%)
Canada 44/46 (95.7%), 5/40 (12.5%)
Tonga 37/39 (94.9%), 3/32 (9.4%)
Argentina 55/58 (94.8%), 10/71 (14.1%)

Tackles (success rate)

South Africa	645 (83.9%)
Argentina	625 (86.9%)
France	612 (89.55%)
England	576 (85.9%)
Fiji	529 (81.3%)

Line breaks (average per match)

New Zealand	30 (6.0)
South Africa	16 (2.3)
England	14 (2.0)
Wales	14 (3.5)
Scotland	13 (2.6)

Errors (average per match)

Argentina	75 (10)
South Africa	67 (9)
France	63 (9)
Scotland	61 (12)
England	68 (13)

Pool A

8 September, Stade Felix Bollaert, Lens
England (21) **28 United States** (3) **10**
Cueto, Lewsey, Noon, Catt (Farrell 63), Robinson (Tait 67), Barkley, Perry (Richards 60), Sheridan, Regan (Chuter 63), Vickery (capt; Stevens 63), Shaw (Corry 63), Kay, Worsley (Moody 69), Rees, Dallaglio
Tries: Robinson, Barkley, Rees
Cons: Barkley (2)
Pens: Barkley (3)

14 September, Stade de France, Saint Denis
England (0) **0 South Africa** (20) **36**
Robinson (Tait 58), Lewsey, Noon (Richards 79), Farrell, Sackey, Catt, Perry (Gomarsall h-t), Sheridan (Freshwater 78), Regan (Chuter 56), Stevens, Shaw (Borthwick 78), Kay, Corry (capt), Rees (Moody 53), Easter

22 September, Stade de Beaujoire, Nantes
England (23) **44 Samoa** (12) **22**
Lewsey, Sackey, Tait (Hipkiss 73), Barkley, Cueto, Wilkinson, Gomarsall, Sheridan (Freshwater 65), Chuter, Stevens, Shaw (Borthwick 65), Kay, Corry (capt), Worsley (Moody 70), Easter
Tries: Corry (2), Sackey (2)

Cons: Wilkinson (3)
Pens: Wilkinson 4
DGs: Wilkinson (2)

28 September, Parc des Princes, Paris
England (19) **36 Tonga** (10) **20**
Lewsey, Sackey (Hipkiss), Tait, Barkley (Farrell 52),
Cueto (Richards 73), Wilkinson, Gomarsall, Sheridan,
Chuter (Mears 67), Stevens (Vickery 57), Borthwick,
Kay, Corry (capt; Dallaglio 65), Moody, Easter
Tries: Sackey (2)
Pens: Wilkinson (2)
DGs: Wilkinson (2)

Quarter-final

6 October, Stade Vélodrome, Marseille
Australia (10) **10 England** (6) **12**
Robinson, Sackey, Tait, Catt (Flood 64), Lewsey,
Wilkinson, Gomarsall, Sheridan, Regan (Chuter 52),
Vickery (capt; Stevens 59), Shaw, Kay, Corry, Moody
(Worsley 66), Easter (Dallaglio 69)
Pens: Wilkinson (4)

Semi-final

13 October, Stade de France, Saint Denis
England (5) **14 France** (6) **9**
Robinson, Sackey, Tait, Catt (Flood 68), Lewsey (Hipkiss
40), Wilkinson, Gomarsall (Richards 70), Sheridan,
Regan (Chuter 65), Vickery (capt; Stevens 56), Shaw,
Kay, Corry, Moody (Worsley 54), Easter (Dallaglio 69)
Try: Lewsey
Pens: Wilkinson (2)
DG: Wilkinson

Final

20 October, Stade de France, Saint Denis
England (3) 6 South Africa (9) 15

Robinson (Hipkiss 47), Sackey, Tait, Catt (Flood 51), Cueto, Wilkinson, Gomarsall, Sheridan, Regan (Chuter 63), Vickery (capt; Stevens 43), Shaw, Kay, Corry, Moody (Worsley 64, Richards 71), Easter (Dallaglio 65)
Pens: Wilkinson

Appearances

7 B. Kay; A. Sheridan; M. Corry (2 tries, 10 pts), N. Easter, M. Tait (1 try, 5 pts), L. Moody, G. Chuter, M. Stevens
6 J. Lewsey (1 try, 5 pts), P. Sackey (4 tries, 20 pts), S. Shaw, A. Gomarsall, J. Wilkinson (5 cons, 14 pens, 5 DGs, 67 pts), P. Richards
5 J. Robinson (1 try, 5 pts), M. Catt, M. Regan, P. Vickery, J. Worsley, L. Dallaglio
4 M. Cueto, D. Hipkiss
3 O. Barkley (1 try, 2 cons, 3 pens, 18 pts), A. Farrell (1 try, 5 pts), S. Borthwick, T. Flood
2 T. Rees (1 try, 5 pts), S. Perry, P. Freshwater
1 L. Mears
0 N. Abendanon

Tries

4 P. Sackey
2 M. Corry
1 O. Barkley, A. Farrell, J. Lewsey, T. Rees, J. Robinson, M. Tait

Top points scored

J. Wilkinson	67 pts
P. Sackey	20 pts
O. Barkley	18 pts
M. Corry	10 pts

The final – match statistics

England		South Africa
1	Line breaks	1
77	Tackles made	81
11	Tackles missed	16
5	Scrums won	9
1	Scrums lost	0
19	Line-outs won on throw	13
7	Line-outs lost on throw	0
4	Turnovers won	4
10	Errors made	8
7	Penalties conceded	5

Possession – 55 per cent England, 45 per cent South Africa

Territory – 57 per cent England, 43 per cent South Africa

There was one other interesting statistic. The two guys who came second over the weekend (the first of the losers, as some unkind people say), Jonny Wilkinson and Lewis Hamilton, are both teetotallers. However, they broke the habit and both had a few jars. Jonny wrote in his column in *The Times* on the Monday after the final:

I suspect that it is widely known that I am teetotal. Well I broke the habit of pretty much a lifetime after the game on Saturday night and had a bit of a blow-out. It was the first time in years and simply seemed the right time and the right thing to do.

A huge bond has been formed in this squad over the past few weeks and I didn't want to break it. After most games here, people have done different things in different groups, but after the final on Saturday, it seemed right to remain as a group, all as close and tight as we have become. I am proud to have been in this team and in this squad and I wanted to show that.

It also helped to be together like that, to get back to the hotel and then go straight out again. Anything, I felt, rather than stop and ruminate on what had gone before. There will be plenty of time, I know, when I'll be feeling the pain of having lost the World Cup final, but our Saturday night was more a case of putting that off. We actually managed to have fun, but I tell you, I certainly felt rank as a result of it.

A friend of mine who works for McLaren told me that Lewis Hamilton felt pretty rank the day after the Brazilian Grand Prix as well.

While Jonny and Lewis were nursing their hangovers, *The Guardian* was full of praise for them and their team-mates, saying in a leader on the Monday morning, under the headline IN PRAISE OF … SPORTING LEGENDS:

Normally it would be fair to say that the worlds of rugby union and Formula One have little in common – beyond the fact that successful practitioners of each have to be masters of their sport's respective black arts. True, other qualities such as team-work, fitness and the ability to accelerate through a gap all play their part in both. It is also undeniable that both sports are overwhelmingly guy things. Most of the time, though, rugby's raw but blokey physicality is a world away from the jetset glamour and hi-tech danger of the motor racing circuit. Yet over the last couple of days many of these differences evaporated, with much of the country (not just England) structuring weekend tasks around Saturday's rugby world cup final and yesterday's last Grand Prix of the F1 season. Patriotic pride was an essential part of the glue that ensured so many cheered on Jonny and the boys in Paris and then Lewis Hamilton in distant Brazil. Another ingredient is that each was such an irresistible story: rugby's once clodhopping no-hopers transforming themselves through pride and guts into potential champions (and if Cueto's try had been given maybe world-beaters too); and the sheer brilliance of motor racing's rookie whose abundance of grace and talent swept so many rivals to finish one point short of the ultimate prize. Of course winning in sport matters, and the weekend defeats are a blow. But these were also ennobling human narratives to inspire even the most sport-resistant.

– France was a winner too –

If the 2007 World Cup was a triumph for South Africa on the pitch, the winners off the pitch were the French supporters and organisers of the tournament. Even before the final, over 2 million people had passed through the turnstiles, including an amazing 48,527 at Parc des Princes for the pool game between Italy and Portugal. The average attendance before the final was 46,714, and the final will have pushed it a little higher. Syd Millar, the outgoing Chairman of the International Rugby Board, said:

This has been the best ever World Cup, I'm quite confident

about that. We've had a magnificent response from the people of France who have come out and supported the event in record attendances. But, more importantly, on the field of play we have had a great festival of rugby. It was a festival more than a competition to some degree especially in the pool stages, so we're very happy with it.

There were people prepared to say that the big loser, apart from New Zealand, was attacking play. And, as it happened, the team that seemed prepared to attack more than any other was New Zealand.

Jonathan Davies, perhaps slightly tongue-in-cheek, wondered in *The Independent on Sunday* whether teams should be reduced from 15 to 13 men by getting rid of the wing-forwards. He wrote:

My opening remark about getting rid of wing-forwards was not quite serious, but with players getting bigger and faster every year the presence of 30 on the park does cause more congestion than the game needs.

When you think of the great flankers we've seen down the years, I'm reluctant to suggest their departure but, while they can be brilliant when going forward, flankers are destructive players. Remove them and thrilling outside-halves might not be a thing of the past.

If you reduce teams to 13 it doesn't mean that you will end up with rugby league. Scrums, line-outs, rucks and mauls will still feature but, with more space available, the quality, attraction and excitement will improve.

He noted that defensive play was already embedded in the English Premiership and was concerned that it might replace the helter-skelter of the Super 14s.

Certainly it was a shame that, in a final watched by 80,000 die-hard enthusiasts in the Stade de France and by millions, even perhaps billions, around the world, there were only three movements to set the pulse racing a little faster and to stick in the memory. We have already covered Mathew Tait's break which so nearly produced that critical England try. For South Africa there was Fourie du Preez making a blind-side run and François Steyn making a great break which took the South Africans to the English try-line. But that was it. The rest was a lot of kicking and forwards crashing into each other with terrifying power and ferocity. There were few of the silky skills associated with running, feinting and passing that make rugby such a wonderful game to watch when they are on display.

Richard Williams, that brilliant journalist in *The Guardian* who can write equally well on football, Formula One or rugby, summed it all up in his usual masterly fashion:

But, oh, the rugby itself. How terrible was that? Those who bought tickets in the hopes of seeing Doug Howlett, Bryan Habana, Paul Sackey or Christophe Dominici scorching down the wings on a regular basis would have been sorely disappointed by what they were offered. Instead they would have acquired a cricked neck as a result of the latest coaching fixation, summed up in the term 'field position'.

It was in the early tournament, when France played Ireland in Saint-Denis, that I got a glimpse – perhaps later than more knowledgeable observers – of what was happening. It was dismal stuff. 'Both sides seemed concerned only to hoist steepling kicks,' I wrote, 'as though the ball could earn them air miles.' Ronan O'Gara and Lionel Beauxis seemed happy to ignore the existence of their talented backs, instead appearing to be engaged in a personal duel to see which of them could be the first man to get the ball into orbit around the earth.

But it was not personal. It was strategic. And before long it became apparent that Bernard Laporte and Eddie O'Sullivan were not the only coaches who believed that the best way to expose chinks in the opposition's defence was to hoist mortar shells at every opportunity.

Laporte was the most blatant offender, using Beauxis in place of Frédéric Michalak and Damien Traille in place of Clément Poitrenaud against the All Blacks and England simply because their ability to kick huge distances made them more valuable to his neanderthal plan than a genuine playmaker in the outside-half position and a real specialist at full-back. It worked, amazingly enough, against an over-confident New Zealand, before becoming drastically unstuck against an England team who, whatever their technical deficiencies, were prepared to fight.

– Final words –

So there we are. What an amazing six weeks it has been. I have always been a rugby nut, so I was enjoying it even in the early stages when England's performances were making most people despair. Nevertheless, I enjoyed it a lot more as England started to play better. It was a wonderful ride upwards as they beat first Samoa, then Tonga and then, wonder of wonders, Australia and France.

Of course it was a shame about the final, and more of a shame, in a way, that both sides were somewhat inhibited in what they were prepared to try.

Finally, three cheers for France for its organisation and the whole atmosphere in which the tournament was played. And three cheers for all the fans, from whichever country. They all behaved well – not impeccably, but certainly without any rancour or the ridiculous, yobbish rowdyism that unfortunately has come to taint international football matches.

ACKNOWLEDGEMENTS

This book needed to be written but it needed to be published if anyone was going to be able to read it and relive the glories achieved by the England team. I am eternally grateful to Icon Books for agreeing to publish it and to do it so quickly. I write long-hand and I am most grateful to Icon's Betty Thompson and her daughter, Karen, for typing my draft the instant they received my scribbles. Icon's Editorial Director, Duncan Heath, in spite of his heavy workload, copy-edited the manuscript immediately and made several valuable recommendations. His team also proof-read the typeset manuscript without delay. I thank them all and the whole of Icon Books for bringing the book to the public within 21 days of the final of the 2007 Rugby World Cup.

Googlies, Nutmegs & Bogeys

The Origins of Peculiar Sporting Lingo

BOB WILSON

Googlies, Nutmegs & Bogeys
The Origins of Peculiar Sporting Lingo
Bob Wilson

Have you ever flashed at a zooter in the corridor of uncertainty while on a sticky dog? Maybe you've seen someone hit a mulligan out of the screws to grab a birdie at Amen Corner?

The world of sport has its own language, wonderfully rich in strange words and phrases, whose origins often stretch back centuries. Veteran BBC presenter and football legend Bob Wilson has written this brilliant illustrated guide to the fascinating true meanings, heritage and evolution of the great sporting terms we use today.

'The daddy of male loo-reading books ... Bob Wilson's compendium should be sent out by right to every lad when he reaches the age of assent, in exactly the same way centurions receive a telegraph from the Queen.'
Scotland on Sunday

'Brilliant. I loved it!'
David Seaman MBE

'Wilson conducts an engaging romp through sport's more colourful terminology ... buy it to be entertained.'
Independent

'A cracking read'
Daily Express

BOB WILSON is the veteran presenter of nine football World Cups, as well as BBC *Grandstand*, *Football Focus*, *Sportsnight* and *Match of the Day*. He also presented the most watched football match in British TV history, with an audience of over 26 million. Bob originally qualified as a teacher before being lured away to play football for Scotland and Arsenal, with whom he won the European Fairs Cup and the League and FA Cup double.

UK £9.99
ISBN: 978-1840467-74-1

The sequel to the bestselling
Googlies, Nutmegs & Bogeys

Rucks, Pucks & Sliders

More Origins of Peculiar Sporting Lingo

BOB WILSON

Rucks, Pucks & Sliders
More Origins of Peculiar Sporting Lingo
Bob Wilson

Why is fighting in a square ring with strange gloves on called boxing? Why is it so difficult to stand up in the Pope's living room? And why does the Prince of Wales dislike buckets of nails and people with wet feet?

Rucks, Pucks & Sliders reveals all as Bob Wilson explores the derivation of another collection of bizarre words and phrases from the wonderfully rich language of sport. Find out why, as a custodian, Bob has spent much of his life trying to keep bananas out of onion bags, why a submarine can often land you in a sin bin, who killed the Galacticos, why snooker balls wipe their feet, and why you'll never see a condor from the Crow's Nest.

Laced with anecdotes from Wilson's own football and television careers, *Rucks, Pucks & Sliders* features one of sport's most enduring icons guiding us through the fascinating true meanings, heritage and evolution of great sporting terms we use today. As Kevin Keegan says, 'It's a lesson in the language of sport from a man that should know.'

BOB WILSON is the veteran presenter of nine football World Cups, as well as BBC *Grandstand*, *Football Focus*, *Sportsnight* and *Match of the Day*. He also presented the most watched football match in British TV history, with an audience of over 26 million. Bob originally qualified as a teacher before being lured away to play football for Scotland and Arsenal, with whom he won the European Fairs Cup and the League and FA Cup double.

UK £9.99
ISBN: 978-1840468-25-0

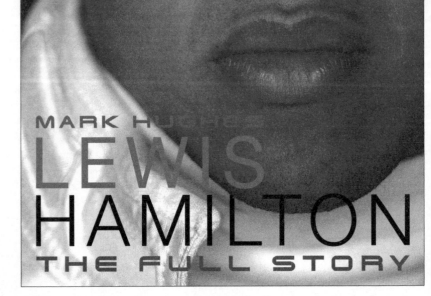

MARK HUGHES
LEWIS
HAMILTON
THE FULL STORY

Lewis Hamilton
The Full Story
Mark Hughes

No driver has ever made such an instant impact on the sport of F1 racing as Lewis Hamilton. The first black Grand Prix driver, his astonishing level of success in his rookie season, together with his swash-buckling, attacking style, has created a sensation. It has also been a central factor in the most exciting and controversial season of F1 in living memory as Hamilton was involved in a three-way fight for the world crown. Industrial espionage, claims of team favouritism and some stunning on-track action have peppered Hamilton's first season in the sport's top category.

Here is the in-depth story of this phenomenon – from his upbringing on a Stevenage council estate to the day he first sat in a kart as a seven-year-old to his sensational challenge on the world title. Friends, colleagues, team-mates, rivals, chaperones and engineers who have worked with him here give some remarkable insights into Lewis the man and the driver, as well as into the close but complex relationship with father Anthony, the man who has largely steered his career. In the process, we see how F1 success has changed this young man's life in a very short space of time.

MARK HUGHES is recognised as one of Formula One's top journalists, and his reports and columns for *Autosport* magazine have won him wide acclaim. ITV and Radio 5 Live regularly benefit from his expertise. He has written a number of books on F1, one of which won the 2005 Illustrated Sports Book of the Year.

In the words of *Motor Sport* magazine: 'None have so effectively combined a passion for and understanding of the human and technical sides of the sport, viewed the political machinations with such wry, subversive humour and informed us so well as to how this affects what happens on the track. He's our own beatnik Kerouac taking the best bits from the journalistic greats and raising the bar for everyone.'

UK £16.99
ISBN: 978-1840468-55-7